How To Be A
MYSTIC
In A
TRAFFIC JAM

Reflections on Living as a Spiritual Person in Everyday Life

Dr. Jodi Prinzivalli

authorHOUSE

1663 LIBERTY DRIVE, SUITE 200
BLOOMINGTON, INDIANA 47403
(800) 839-8640
www.authorhouse.com

First published by AuthorHouse 07/29/04

ISBN: 1-4184-0747-X (e)
ISBN: 1-4184-0749-6 (sc)
ISBN: 1-4184-0748-8 (dj)

Printed in the United States of America
Bloomington, Indiana

This book is printed on acid-free paper.

Dr. Jodi Prinzivalli
Center for Healing and Energetic Psychology
70 Hilltop Road
Ramsey, NJ 07446

To order books or for information
visit our websites at:
www.energeticpsychology.com
www.interfaith-encounter.org

E-mail: jodiprinz@optonline.net
Phone: 201.851.4909

Design by Lyndie Kahanek

"This is a remarkable book and we are very pleased to strongly recommend it to the reading public. The author tackles the issue that so many of us are trying to solve. How does one live a spiritual life in a very busy and very harassed technological society? Dr. Prinzivalli has a very extensive background as a therapist and as a spiritual teacher and what she writes comes out of her own experience in working with these profound opposites. It is beautifully written and cannot help but support the life and work of anyone doing psychospiritual work of any kind."

Hal Stone, PhD and Sidra Stone, PhD
Originators of the Voice Dialogue Process
Authors of *Embracing Our Selves;*
Embracing Each Other; and
Healing the Inner Critic

Table of Contents

SECTION V: SPIRITUAL TEACHERS

SECTION VI: THE FEMALE MYSTIC

ACKNOWLEDGEMENTS

It has been said that there is nothing original under the sun, and yet every moment is a new creation. This book is an unfoldment of all that I have learned over the course of my life, but there are four teachers in particular who have had a profound impact on what I believe about life, God, relationships and healing. It is hard to separate what is from me and what is from them, as most of what I write is a personal weaving of something I have learned from one or all of them. These four are Jason Shulman, (renowned healer and originator of Integrated Kabbalistic Healing), Sidra Stone and Hal Stone (originators of the Voice Dialogue process), and Alexis Johnson (one of the best psychotherapists I have ever met). I feel blessed to have studied with these four people and their mentorship continues to influence my life on a daily basis.

I also want to thank Karen Gerdean Bowen for her writing skills and Lyndie Kahanek, graphic artist extraordinaire. Their editing and technical feedback were invaluable to me.

In addition there are a few others who I must thank. The first is Bill Prinzivalli, whose generous heart and patient soul has earned him points in heaven through eternity. To my Mom and Dad, whose lives are a living example of selfless service, unwavering faith and eternal flexibility. Their ability to never give up hope has repeatedly proven that miracles can happen in the face of overwhelming odds. Also to my family, Wendy, Peter, Bob, Bren, Jeanne, Chris, Rosalie, Fran and Joe, who have provided the family love and nourishment that I cherish. To Larry, Monica, George, Laurie and David, who each in their own way have given me unique inspiration, friendship and support. And to my little pumpkins, Isabelle and Teddy, who are simply the lights of my life.

x

AUTHOR'S NOTE

This book is a composition of articles, teachings and reflections which were written over the course of about 10 years. In keeping with the theme of practical mysticism, it is designed to be practical in its reading. Each chapter is self-contained, yet there are many common themes. As such, this book can be read in many ways. You can read a single short chapter in a few minutes as you are waiting for the kids, or sitting on the subway. You can read from back to front, open the book randomly on any day, or read every word from start to finish. Whatever your style, may you find comfort and strength in these words and find useful tools for living in the challenging times we face every day.

Jodi Prinzivalli
New York City, NY
August 2004

SECTION I: INTRODUCTION TO PRACTICAL MYSTICISM

What Is a Mystic?

We live in an unusual time, a time when spiritual seekers sit side by side with politicians and business people. Often they are one in the same. Some find solace in traditional religion while others embrace concepts of the New Age. Yet there are many who cannot find harmony with their current path. For those who still search for a spiritual path that resonates with their soul, this is an invitation to explore the possibilities of a practical mysticism grounded in everyday life.

To begin, it is important to redefine what a mystic in our modern day truly looks like. Though Webster's dictionary may have its own definition, for the sake of clarity, I want to present an alternative definition for those of us striving to live a meaningful and conscious life.

A mystic is anyone who believes in the unseen world, who believes there is something greater than what meets the eye in this world, and who desires to understand it. A mystic is one who believes that everything happens for a reason, and that there is an organizing intelligence behind all that occurs. A mystic is one who uses both the logic of the mind and the intuition of the soul to make decisions about how to live life. A mystic does not have to be religious or belong to any religious sect.

There are many ways to practice mysticism in outer behavior. The unifying factor is the belief in a greater existence beyond the physical world. In America alone, we have mystics in science and physics, in biotech labs and computer software companies. We have mystics in synagogues, churches, mosques and temples everywhere. But as we all know, just showing up at one of those places does not a mystic make.

Although an individual may choose a particular mystical tradition to study, practical mysticism affirms that no one tradition is better than another. The fundamentals of practical mysticism dictate that this decision is made by the truth of the soul. If one chooses a path based on coercion or the beliefs of others, there is a betrayal of the soul at the highest level. If one takes on a path that is deeply felt as the truth of the heart, then this path can never be wrong. A true mystic will always allow for their own personal truth as well as that of another, even if it is "different." A true mystic knows that these differences are only on the outer level and that they disappear as we approach our core or inner levels. As one person may prefer the color purple and another, green, individual souls have tastes and preferences in the path of their spirit. It is essential to honor these qualities and allow space and permission for the discovery of the best home for the soul.

For a mystic, actions are imperative in the world. A mystic believes that every action has a ripple effect across the universe, that right action can heal a person, a family, a nation or a planet, though only within the timing and will of the Creator. A mystic knows that no act of kindness is lost, though its benefits may take years to reap. And a mystic knows that even thoughts can affect change, that the mind is the creator, and as we think, so shall it be.

Although the use of labels can be limiting, we need language to communicate. Within my own journey, I have walked through the mystical paths of Christianity (A Course in Miracles and Alice Bailey's teachings), Islam (Sufism), Hindu (the Yogic tradition), Tantra and the mystical path of Judaism (the Kabbalah). If I were asked today what my spiritual path is, I would say that I am a Jewish Kabbalist who loves and appreciates Sufism. This would probably raise the protests of many purists in the world. And there is absolutely a place for pure mystical teachings. Many souls are purely of one resonance. But others of us live in many worlds. The time has come for each of us to find our own path, our own tradition that works within the perfection of our unique soul. We must create a safe vessel and find like-minded community which can also tolerate differences in outer expression. Just because I prefer purple and you prefer green, does not mean we cannot share a meal together, or dance or even pray our individual prayers together. It does not mean that purple is better than green or green is better than purple. It also does not mean we must combine purple and green into one watered-down amalgam of tradition. The differences are as important as the similarities.

This is the essence of mysticism—living practically and responsibly in the world; having an abundant life and mastery of the physical realm, while honoring the unseen worlds and the Divine intelligence behind it all; honoring all paths as leading to the same place, none higher than the other except on a personal resonance level; being willing to explore the hidden energies and unconscious drives that make up our human struggles and suffering, while being willing to embrace them in their original intent to help us; remaining self-responsible for the results in our life; being willing to courageously examine the truth of our heart and act on it even when faced with the displeasure and misunderstanding of other people; trusting in the greater good of all things and the wisdom of the voice of truth inside, willing to ride the currents of life as they lead us to the next step along the path.

Whether you wear a robe or a business suit, whether you eat vegetables or buffalo wings, the inner landscape is what defines a mystic. Regardless of religion, practice, profession or culture, mysticism is about what is on the inside and the reflection of that in daily lifestyle, words and deeds. The rest is personal preference.

Holding Two Things at the Same Time

What is the difference between the average person and one who shines brightly in the world? Though the answer is complex, a few clues exist in response to this question. One such clue is this—the one who shines has both a clear vision and the resources, internal and external, to accomplish it. Practical mystics are such people. They are individuals who believe in the goodness of humanity. They know there is something greater than themselves operating in this world, while remaining grounded in the realities of physical existence. Practical mystics live their lives with realism but with purpose. They acknowledge and accept the human condition as fallible and imperfect, yet capable of greatness. They do not lose sight of the grand possibilities, while at the same time they live life in a practical manner that allows for the duality of existence.

This is not an easy task. It requires the ability to hold the tension of opposites, to know that life is messy and cannot be put into a nice neat package. It requires the courage to live in this messiness of life without illusion but also without despair. The grandest lifework is learning to hold the duality of the physical world, and the unity of the spiritual world at the same time—denying neither, neglecting neither, allowing for the existence of both and not shattering in the process.

We must constantly walk the balance between self-inquiry and service in the world, between becoming self-absorbed and avoiding vulnerability. There is only one way to negotiate this middle way, and that is the path of self-responsibility. If we are ever to live in a world of coexistence and peace, then self-responsibility must be the prevailing theme of life. Such self-responsibility requires the willingness to blame no one, including ourselves and an unwillingness to become a victim to life's unpredictable and often seemingly unjust circumstances. We must empower ourselves to have choice regardless of the circumstances that come our way. We must have the equanimity to trust the Divine Intelligence which may have a grander plan.

A Sufi story is told about Moses and his teacher, a prophet named al-Khidr. Moses went to al-Khidr and asked to be taught the secrets of the universe. Al-Khidr agreed with one condition—that Moses was to follow him and not question any action that he took. Moses agreed, but soon found himself in a quandary when al-Khidr behaved in a seemingly "unspiritual" way with the local townspeople. Later it was revealed that had this action not been taken, the entire town would have been destroyed. But Moses did not know this, and only saw what he judged as an incorrect action. Al-Khidr sent him away. Thus in his shortsightedness and lack of vision of the higher picture, he lost the opportunity of the moment. We each do this in our own smaller ways all the time.

Yossi Klein Halevi, a gifted writer, philosopher, and journalist in the Holy Land says, "To feel God's presence in meditation and prayer is the easy part. The real challenge is to feel God's presence in failure—and even more in the seeming failure of a job done for God." Those of us who dedicate our lives to God experience this reality repeatedly in our lives. We do our best but sometimes it appears that we fail. Who is to say in the final analysis what is true—whether an apparent failure is not in fact an aspect of a greater plan for good? But usually we have no way of knowing. Can we accept this fact? Can we dedicate our lives to living practically in the world, having deep faith in the Divine Order, and not asking for so-called success or judging our actions based on their immediate results? Great fortitude is required to do this, to say the least. Inherent in this fortitude is the essence and paradox of practical mysticism. We must follow the guidance of our heart, the Voice of Truth, even when it takes us in directions that may appear illogical, even when others may not be happy about our decisions. At the same time, we must also have the courage to self-correct if we get feedback that indicates we are not going in the best direction.

The middle way. The practical mystic. Enjoyment of the world, enjoyment of the body, enjoyment of life's pleasures, without becoming self-absorbed, preoccupied or neglectful. Chant God's name and pay the bills. Say a blessing and take the kids to soccer practice. Pray the morning prayer and invest in the stock market. This is the work at hand. We walk the balance beam of the center path without disowning anything. In this way, the lost sparks are embraced and returned to their root in the Divine through the living of our daily life. And in the end, we cannot evaluate the meaning of our life based on immediate results. As a dear friend of mine used to say, "only God knows and She ain't telling."

The Spectrum of Love and Power

Living as a practical mystic requires the ability to hold and tolerate the "tension of the opposites." The Middle Way means standing at the center and consciously choosing, after having explored both sides completely. As human beings, we have a tendency to want to resolve our anxiety by choosing one side or disowning the other in order to experience relief. But this relief is at best temporary, and truly an illusion. Inevitably the energy of the other side begins to build again.

One very important spectrum of opposites in this dynamic is the spectrum of love and power. Individuals who are primarily based in the material world tend to utilize power to gain what they want in order to alleviate their anxiety, often at the expense of love, connection and fulfilling relationships.

But spiritually-identified people are equally imbalanced if they always insist on thinking positive thoughts, focusing only on love and light, seeing power as bad or unspiritual. Both of these extremes are equally destructive in their own way and can lead to great challenges if not brought to conscious awareness. Every beautiful creation in the world, even the creation of a new life, requires both love and power. Love is the sustaining essence, but power is the life force, the movement, the action in the world. Power is the creative energy that builds the vision. Love without right use of power leads to spiritual glamour, illusion and ungroundedness, while power without love leads to an empty heart.

If we disown our power sides, they will be expressed in more and more hidden ways. Many variations on this theme can be found, from acting out the shadow in secretive ways to the use of judgement and criticism in an attempt to create a boundary. Judgement becomes a false substitute for power, and rather than creating a protective boundary, it creates anxiety, fear, self-hatred, worry and doubt which separates us in an illusionary way from the perceived problem. Right use of power, on the other hand, eliminates the need for extreme judgement and criticism. Power says, "No thank you." Period. It is neutral. There is no hatred, no criticism, no judgement, just "no."

Power in general has been given a bad wrap. Spiritual people frequently judge power as bad because it is too often used in its extreme without the balancing force of love. But every sacred text known to man is filled with stories about the powerful side of the Divine. We cannot reconcile this by turning our backs on the sacred text and, as Carl Jung says, creating figures of light in our minds. This only pushes things further underground. Some of us cringe at the thought of such power being written into a sacred text or we rationalize the writing as a document for a different time or generation. But in reality, every great mystical teaching has various qualities of God that are about strength and might, power and destruction. The Kabbalistic Tree of Life *(see diagram on page 13)* has a Mercy side of the tree, a Severity side of the tree and a Central channel. All three columns in equal balance are what define well-being in this modality. So why is it that we have such difficulty with the power aspects of the Divine? Probably because we see them used and abused in the world without the balance of love and mercy. But this does not make power unspiritual, it makes it imbalanced. Cancer is the perfect example of this. The lack of a destroyer quality in the illness results in the overgrowth of a life-taking cell. Use of a destroyer quality, be it chemotherapy or psychic surgery, is what provides the healing. In fact, I have often wondered what would happen to the cancer rate if there were more teaching and permission around right use of power and the divinity of the destroyer quality in its balanced form.

If we are to be practical mystics, we must make peace with the fact that we live in the physical world, a world that requires the right use of power in order to heal and survive. We cannot just escape to the mountaintop. We must live with our feet on the ground and look life squarely in the eye. Yes, with mercy, yes with love...and also with Divine Power and the ability to say "no" and have clear and direct boundaries. We must walk the terrain of understanding the disowned power voices within us, or we risk the possibility of those streams being expressed in much more difficult and traumatic ways. If we do not explore our own instinctual power aspects in a conscious manner, we will have to hide them and find ways to cover them over to keep them from being known to both ourselves and the people in our lives. Yet if we explore these aspects with our eyes wide open, we can come into the center and truly create a strong vessel capable of carrying the tension of the opposites. We will find we do not need to choose one or the other, but can remain in the center, embracing both, seeing the value in both and utilizing those qualities in amounts that fit the situation appropriately—without feeling that the power streams are bad or need to be somehow eliminated, which in fact is not a possibility, at least on this earth.

Power with love is the most life-affirming, life-giving quality we can embody and manifest. Only when we can value the exquisite creative force that power brings, the safety of the "no" that power brings, the ability to protect and take care of that which we love and cherish, can we be practical mystics living in the modern world of the 21st century. Most exquisitely, when we have permission for a complete "no," we also have the capacity for a complete "yes" when the time is right We have the opportunity to open our hearts completely and be in intimate contact with ourselves and our loved ones. Knowing we are fully capable of a "no" allows us to be fully capable of "yes" in its most complete way.

Regarding the secretive life or the parts of ourselves that we push away, only compassion will heal. A shadow unexplored is always a gem seeking right expression. Secrets occur when there is no vessel in the consciousness for them to be contained, nowhere for them to be explored with love and safety. Every secret is a protective drive for safety. Every hidden acting out, every impulsive addictive behavior, is in fact a disowned part seeking healing. The gradual and compassionate exploration of these parts of ourselves actually carries the deepest opportunities for connection and wholeness. And almost always, the most hidden aspects are the instinctual and power-based energies which have been judged and criticized away, being banished to the closet only to percolate like a pressure cooker for their inevitable expression in more disconnected ways. By being willing to explore that which we most want to hide, we find the hidden gems of our true nature which could be expressed in a different way if we understood their positive purpose. By judging something as "wrong" and pushing it underground, we lose a chance for wholeness and for reclaiming deeper aspects of who we really are.

As we evolve as a planet, the side of love/mercy and the side of severity/power will come together in the center, a balance which exists in the higher realms of spirit. But we do not live there and we must not confuse the higher realms of spirit with the realms of the physical world. We must develop the capacity to hold the worlds of the unity and the worlds of duality at the same time, not either/or, not better or worse, just at the same time. This creates a third state, something which Jason Shulman, renowned healer and innovator of Integrated Kabbalistic Healing, calls the Third Thing—a state that is neither of unity or of duality but which can hold both at the same time, a state that understands both and allows for living in a manner that is productive, nourishing, satisfying and creative.

For as long as we live in a physical body, we are rooted in the life of duality. To ignore that fact is the cause of great suffering, illness, turmoil and misunderstanding. But there is another possibility. That possibility is to live in the world of duality by going into our hearts, bringing all the beauty and love that we have inside, wrapping it around our Divine, God-given power and being lovingly direct when it is time to say "no thanks." We must have this internal permission when something does not feel right, safe or in the highest good for ourselves or our family. Our inner heart always knows the truth...always. We must learn to differentiate between our lower self impulses and the true heart, and once we know that, to have the great courage to listen, to act, or to lovingly say, "I don't think that's a good idea." When we have the full ability to say "no," we also have the full ability to say "yes." This gives us the capacity to live in the world of duality while experiencing the world of unity in a safe and healthy vessel.

The Tree of Life Diagram

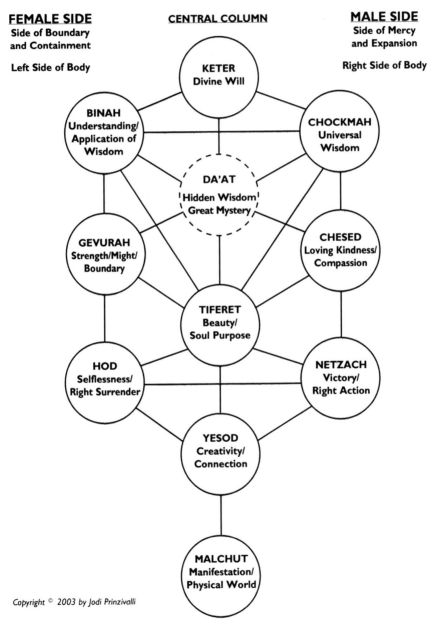

FEMALE SIDE
Side of Boundary
and Containment

Left Side of Body

CENTRAL COLUMN

MALE SIDE
Side of Mercy
and Expansion

Right Side of Body

KETER
Divine Will

BINAH
Understanding/
Application of
Wisdom

CHOCKMAH
Universal
Wisdom

DA'AT
Hidden Wisdom
Great Mystery

GEVURAH
Strength/Might/
Boundary

CHESED
Loving Kindness/
Compassion

TIFERET
Beauty/
Soul Purpose

HOD
Selflessness/
Right Surrender

NETZACH
Victory/
Right Action

YESOD
Creativity/
Connection

MALCHUT
Manifestation/
Physical World

God Is Like a Power Tool

A young client of mine came in recently stating he was confused about spirituality. Turned off by the dogma of his childhood religion, but knowing that something was behind this amazing universe, he was looking for a way to express it. As he started to describe his struggle with the unseen and how to speak about his belief in the Divine Intelligence, an analogy hit me. God—and living a spiritual life—is like a power tool!

Just as electricity is an invisible source of power that we plug into but cannot see, so too is the Divine a source of power that cannot be viewed with the physical eyes. But we can see the results. Just as a carpentry tool requires a power source in order to work, a soul requires the capacity to plug into this Divine Power, even though it cannot be seen. In this regard, it is not important if we "believe in" electricity. It is just there, like the sun on a cloudy day. Just because we cannot see it, does not mean it is not there. We have hundreds of examples of the unseen in our world, from radio waves, to x-rays, to the ever-present cell phone that accompanies us everywhere. In fact, the invisible, and the energy of the invisible, powers up our entire life in the third millennium.

So too, if we only plug into electricity on the physical level but do not plug into the Divine power on a soul level, we will experience a profound emptiness, a sense of meaninglessness in life. The depression that some people experience is often the result of being unable to access or connect to this Divine source. In order for us to live a life of meaning and of purpose, we MUST have an ideology that works, a way to make sense out of the unexplainable in our world, a way to understand why bad things happen to good people and what death is and what our purpose is here on earth.

Divine Intelligence is not something that can be held in your hand (though some spiritual leaders have claimed to be able to do this!). But it can be seen in results, in the manifestation, in the change of life or presence that happens in people. If we are struggling with "believing," then we must ask for the eyes to see. We must see in the same way that we use our cell phones every day. Very few of us would say that we do not "believe in" cell phones and their operation. Yet the same must be true for the spiritual and energetic realms as well.

On the other hand, just plugging in is only half the story.

If we want to build a house, we must plug in the equipment and then we must do the work. God does not "come down" and do it for us. We must put in the time and the effort, while simultaneously being plugged into an eternal source of energy and spiritual nourishment. Otherwise, the result is the same loss and emptiness. We are in charge of our actions, our words, and our behavior. Only we can do the work of our lives, only we can show up for life and take part in what we are here to do. How tragic it is when someone spends their life waiting…waiting for God, waiting for something to change so that they can finally be happy, waiting for the right job or the right relationship in order to begin living their life.

The Divine Source can provide sustenance, energy and support, but we must take the actions…even when those actions are difficult. The results speak for themselves, as they are felt inside on a profound level. You cannot taste the sweetness of the honey by looking at it, but only by putting a drop in your mouth. So too, in the doing, much of the understanding happens. We cannot be given in advance the satisfaction of a house well-built. We cannot know before we pick up the power tool. We can only taste the sweetness of right action by, as Eleanor Roosevelt once said, doing the thing we think we cannot do. In that process, we experience wholeness.

So for a practical mystic, there are two parts of the spiritual life. First we must plug into the Source through all the spiritual tools we know of, then we must do the work at hand. Only doing one side will never be enough for the one who wishes to be awake and conscious. For a practical mystic, living a spiritual life requires both. First we have to plug in through prayer, meditation, retreat and all the spiritual practices that renew us, then we must get to work through our actions and words in the world. For it is right action grounded in a spiritual life, combined with work with the unconscious parts of ourselves, that truly will allow for change that has constancy and meaning.

Our deepest fear is not that we are inadequate.
Our deepest fear is that we are powerful beyond measure.
It is our light, not our darkness that most frightens us.
We ask ourselves, Who am I to be brilliant, gorgeous, talented, fabulous?
Actually, who are you not to be?
You are a child of God.
Your playing small does not serve the world.
There is nothing enlightened about shrinking so that other
people will not feel insecure around you.
We are all meant to shine, as children do.
We were born to make manifest the glory of God that is within us.
It is not just in some of us; it is in everyone.
And as we let our own light shine, we unconsciously give other people
permission to do the same.
As we are liberated from our own fear,
our presence automatically liberates others.

—Marianne Williamson
from A Return To Love:
Reflections on the Principles
of A Course In Miracles

SECTION II: RELATIONSHIP AND SELF-INQUIRY

The Vertical Versus the Horizontal Path

Many years ago, I heard my long-term mentors Hal and Sidra Stone, speak about enlightened teachers and cancer. While it would seem logical that a spiritual master would have control over their own death process, many great teachers have contracted debilitating forms of cancer. On that day years ago, Hal and Sidra, the originators of the psychospiritual process called Voice Dialogue, spoke about the difference between enlightenment and consciousness. They stated that a person can be very enlightened but quite unconscious about their own shadow aspects, the inner landscape that drives behavior and gives motive to the actions and words of an individual. Spiritual work draws in and invokes Divine light. But if an individual has not done their personality work, this light only gives more charge to the unconscious energies existing in the recesses of the self, resulting in greater difficulty for the aspirant on any spiritual path.

That day was the beginning of my own understanding of the need for both the vertical and the horizontal work in the process of spiritual development. Enlightenment is a vertical attainment to God that goes directly between the heart and soul of an individual into union with the Divine Source. But consciousness involves the horizontal work in the world, the awareness of the self, and the dynamics of the shadow and childhood wounding. It involves the willingness to work out patterns that drive behavior in the world that are primarily operating from the unconscious mind. Without this work, these unconscious drives will express themselves in more destructive and harmful ways. The essential imperative is that we do our shadow work as we walk as spiritual beings in the world. Otherwise, the fragile needs of the wounded self will use spirituality as another ground of expression, resulting in emotional imbalance, physical disease and general life turmoil despite whatever spiritual work may have been done. When we are aware of the horizontal pole, we can prevent such imbalance by taking one step into the unconscious every time we make a spiritual leap. Many good tools exist for this kind of work. While my personal favorite is the Voice Dialogue process, any skill that works with the unconscious mind will do. The important thing is to remain willing to do our personality work even as we evolve spiritually and never to think that we have "arrived" or "attained completion."

Often as one grows spiritually, the ego becomes more and more masterful, using even spirituality as a means to avoid personality work. The most recent term for this is "spiritual bypass." If we believe we should "be over this" by now, or we have done so much work that personality difficulties should not plague us any more, we are not only in illusion, but most likely we are pushing underground some wonderfully rich material for our own journey of self-inquiry. As we become more spiritually aware, we also develop the capacity to "dress things up in white" and use even our spiritual path as a justification for difficulties and suffering.

For as long as we are alive in a physical form, there is always more horizontal work to do. And the playground for the horizontal work is within our relationships. It is within relationships that we can discover the hidden parts of ourselves, as the people around us give us daily feedback about the places which need work. Our family and friends all trigger us and provide an opportunity to look at what has been pushed underground. Any form of emotional reactivity is the yellow light. If we are willing to listen to the world and the people around us, we have the opportunity to turn and look at our subconscious and unconscious energies, giving us an eternal source of material for our own development. In this way, relationship is our teacher more than any book or spiritual path. The challenge is to use it in this way.

The prophet Muhammad gave an invaluable clue when he said that our best source of personal growth lies in the criticism of our detractors. If we can take 30% of the criticism we receive as true, we will have a lifetime of material for our own edification and we will never lull ourselves into believing that there is no more personality work to be done. But he stated 30% and not 90%. Our challenge must be to know that others are operating with their own unconscious patterns as well. We must take our 30% and leave the rest for others to work out for themselves. In this way, the information we receive from the people who surround us on a daily basis becomes an eternal resource for self-improvement.

Sex, Chess and Torah

A few years ago, I decided to learn the game of chess. Though the challenge continues, a profound dynamic stood out from the very first lesson. This dynamic goes far beyond the game of chess, and addresses the heart of the matter in relationships between men and women. As it turns out, the game of chess seems to provide a model for how men and women could have beautiful, fulfilling and profound relationships. It goes like this. In the game of chess, the King is the most important, but the Queen has the most power...a striking paradigm for relationship. In fact, most happy couples I know seem to embody this dynamic. And because it is an archetype, the same concept can apply equally to both gay and straight couplehood. The archetype of the male and the female qualities are always a balanced complement, regardless of gender.

One of the unfortunate realities of our society is that from early on, men are encouraged to gather as much power as possible to themselves and women are taught to help them attain that end. The tragic result is men who are overstressed, overworked and unfulfilled, and women who are disempowered and victimized. No one wins in this scenario. On the other hand, if we could make a simple but difficult adjustment, we might discover some very interesting shifts. Rather than attempting to gain power by emasculating our men (or even acting like a man in certain circumstances), what if the women of the world began to embody the dynamic of powerful women who love men? What if we were to understand that right relationship involves honoring our men as the most important aspect of our lives and at the same time be willing to be powerful? In contradiction to what we may have learned (and usually in a very indirect way), whether you are a man or a woman, the opposite sex is not the enemy. Our belief system is.

We truly need to change our paradigm if we are to have successful and happy relationships during this amazing time in which we live. We must begin to shift our lives so that men can be freed of their burden and women can stop feeling victimized. The answer to victimization is not to become a perpetrator. The answer to stress and exhaustion is not to grab more power or to tyrannize the other. Rather, our solutions show up in working with the sides of ourselves that have been taught a lie. This lie exists in regards to power, self-esteem and right relationship.

One of the many ways that individuals grab power is through the use of criticism. For example, one night as I sat in a local restaurant, I observed the young wife of a man basically criticize every word he said until he ultimately withdrew into silence. She then displayed an expression of victory, as if her tirade had actually won her the power she so anxiously was seeking. What she actually got was a withdrawn beloved who will probably, over time, begin to pull away from her and be truly unable to nourish or give her the true power she could have in another circumstance.

At another table was an obviously successful man, meticulously dressed and engaged in a lively conversation with the hostess. After she left, he turned to his date and suggested to her that the loss of a few pounds would make her more attractive to him. This was a beautiful woman with a wonderful figure. But his comment was not meant as truth, it was meant to put her in an inferior place. Had the hostess been his date, he would have said the same thing to her. Again, the power remained imbalanced no matter which conversation we speak about, and the variations on this theme abound.

The alternative is to take a step back and look at our ideas about power and control. Power is not a good thing or a bad thing. It is simply the ability to take action to affect change. What we seek is the middle way, the way that allows the women of the world to honor our men as the most important people in our lives, while we utilize the God-given power we have been given to create, decide and act in the world in a positive and life-affirming way.

A beautiful model of this is found within the Tree of Life in Kabbalah which was spoken about in Chapter 4 (*see diagram on page 13*). This tree is a map of the unseen realm, having a male side, a female side, and a central column. Converse to many of our cultural teachings, the female side includes the quality of strength, might and power, while the male balancing force provides the quality of sweetness and unconditional love. In this worldview, the man brings sweetness to the woman and the woman brings discipline and structure to the man. Though the lower self can misconstrue these ideas, in their truest nature they embody the same aspects as the King and Queen in the game of chess. When a man allows himself to give over power to his mate and when the woman knows how to use it well—to honor, cherish, create and direct (rather than denigrate and emasculate in an attempt to gain power due to anger and frustration), a new dynamic begins to flow forth. The life force of right relationship, sexual energy and passion, self-fulfillment and joy takes root in very slow and subtle ways. Though we must go against the tide of what we have learned, the payoff is rich with rewards.

Can we truly have great relationships without this balance? Perhaps the game of chess and the wisdom of the sages provide us with some genuine alternatives. In a practical and everyday manner, the idea of the King as the most important and the Queen as the most powerful is a rich and rewarding model for how we might have relationships that truly bring us happiness, pleasure and fulfillment.

You Love Me

In the context of our modern lives, many of us have become confused about the nature of service and the nature of giving. We have been taught that giving to another, or helping, or healing means giving up our life energy. We have been taught that a "good" person "gives to others" and does "good things" for others. In their truest definitions, this is exactly what the sacred texts and great teachers of the world have been saying for many centuries. But somewhere along the way it seems we have lost our understanding of what "giving" really is. Ironically, there is a very different way to understand giving. What if giving has nothing to do with fixing, changing or helping another, but rather receiving the love of another that is hidden in their own heart?

This is one of the paradoxes of practical mysticism—that in relationship, the "giver" should receive as much as the "receiver." In this paradigm, giving and receiving are the same.

The secret to this process is to reverse the usual concept of giving and receiving. To know in fact, that we heal another by breathing in the love in their being, and by drawing out the Divine Light that is inherent in each soul, whether it is apparent or not. By consciously breathing in the love from the other, we draw out their capacity to love in a different way.

Rather than saying, "I love you," we say, "You love me." We call forward the other's capacity to love, and to heal the world and themselves by shining our light on the light already in them. We reverse the direction normally considered the way of loving kindness and receive not only a healing, but a deeper level of contact with the other.

Love, healing, connection, or contact in relationship should never be depleting. If it is, we are misunderstanding something. Love is like the perpetual motion machine. It generates more energy as it continues, not less.

In this way, we are nourished in our relationships with each other by receiving the beauty, joy and love in the other, even when it is not on the surface. Even if it is not readily available, we know and believe that in every human being the capacity to love deeply is inherent. Therefore, as a practical mystic, we trust that these qualities are there just waiting to be released from their prison of a broken or hardened heart. But we do not push. We patiently and lovingly just go beyond the outer shell, connect with the light that is already in them and receive it into ourselves. We become their vessel which sometimes shows them what they cannot see themselves. And the most beautiful gift we can give anyone is the gift of receiving him or her in their greatness and their beauty, even when they themselves cannot. We draw it out. And in drawing it out, we are renewed and filled in our own being. By saying, "You love me," the Divine spark is given a conductor and the circle of love is given a kick-start into existence.

Practical mysticism is about reversing the flow, thinking in paradoxes and being able to contain all the contradictions of life by holding the presence of opposites. When we are involved with real human beings, we must learn to think, act and love in different ways than we have been taught, and be willing to go out on the edge for the sake of finding a different way to be in the world with ease and contentment. By giving through receiving, by saying, "You love me," rather than "I love you," we do just that.

…The Skin Horse had lived longer in the nursery than any of the others. He was so old that his brown coat was bald in patches and showed the seams underneath, and most of the hairs in his tail had been pulled out to make string bead necklaces. He was wise, for he had seen a long succession of mechanical toys arrive to boast and swagger, and by-and-by break their mainsprings and pass away, and he knew that they were only toys, and would never turn into anything else. For nursery magic is very strange and wonderful, and only those playthings that are old and wise and experienced like the Skin Horse understand all about it.

"What is Real?" asked the Rabbit one day, when they were laying side-by-side near the nursery fender, before Nana came into the room. "Does is mean having things that buzz inside you and a stick-out handle?"

"Real isn't how you are made," said the Skin Horse. "It's a thing that happens to you. When a child loves you for a long, long time, not just to play with but really loves you, then you become Real."

"Does it hurt?" asked the Rabbit.

"Sometimes," said the Skin Horse, for he was always truthful. "When you are Real you don't mind being hurt."

"Does it happen all at once, like being wound up," he asked, "or bit by bit?"

"It doesn't happen all at once," said the Skin Horse. "You become. It takes a long time. That's why it doesn't often happen to people who break easily or who have sharp edges, or who have to be carefully kept. Generally, by the time you are Real, most of your hair has been loved off, and your eyes drop out and you get loose in the joints and very shabby. But these things don't matter at all, because once you become Real, you can't be ugly, except to people who don't understand."

— The Velveteen Rabbit
Harper Books
1961

Voice of Truth

If you follow the present day world, you will turn your back on The Way.

— Takuan Soho, Zen master advising a
Persian warrior and spiritual leader

If there is one essential quality of a practical mystic, it is the quality of unwavering affirmation of the Voice of Truth in the heart. Though life around us pulls us in a myriad of directions, and the people around us have many wishes and opinions about what we should do and who we should be, the courageous path less traveled is the path of listening to the heart.

Many in our world are ready to tell us what we need to do. They believe they know what is right for us better than ourselves. We have been taught to ignore the inner voice, to give more credit to what is outside of us than what is inside of us. Tragically, that direction often leads us to unhappiness and discomfort. Sometimes it leads to disease, addiction and severe resentment. Always, it is a betrayal of the soul. For there can be only one person who lives our life, and that is ourselves. There is only one individual who truly knows. No one, no matter how much they love us or appear to understand us, can know what it is like to live in our shoes. We are the only ones who have to get up every morning and live the life we have chosen. And even if it does not feel like a choice, that is only because we have not chosen. We have allowed the world to determine for us what our lives will be.

Yet, hope prevails. With every day, there is a new opportunity to choose differently, to listen to what our heart is telling us is good and right for us. This does not mean we should act on lower-self impulses, but on giving validation to what we know is right, an act which takes tremendous courage in this world. The one who walks to his own drum certainly stands out from the rest. And in a world where community depends on conformity, and where conformity demands standardization, even mediocrity, it is too easy to lose ourselves for the sake of fitting in. When we trade our individual self for the sake of community, even the community suffers.

But what kind of community would we create if the norms were to listen to personal truth, regardless of what it looks like? What if we began to value truth over conformity? Then the possibility of a different type of community might begin to emerge, one where everyone is responsible for their own truth, and for listening to what is right for them, even if they disagree with those around them.

This level of social value also requires a willingness to let go of the need to be right. We live in a time when, unfortunately, being right is often regarded as more important than being loved. Ironically, being right is so subjective that, in reality, it doesn't even exist. We must develop the capacity to tolerate a differing viewpoint and see it as equally right, valid and important. We need to be able to have our own truth and allow another to have theirs as well, even if it appears different than our own.

As we all have seen in the mass psychology of the great holocaust and genocides of the twentieth century, consensus does not necessarily imply truth. As individuals, we must be able to stand for our own truth, even if it means some relationships will fade, even if it means we no longer share certain things. But if we can allow this in each other, then we can learn to disagree without experiencing a broken heart and without going to battle. Our dear ones can go their own way and we can still love each other. We can still be beloveds of the heart, even if we now attend different houses of worship or read different books.

This is another challenge of the day—to turn toward the Way by not having to comply with every message of the present-day world. By doing so, we create a different world. And in that world, the Way and the Truth of our hearts are the same. No one has to be pushed out of our lives, even if they choose a different road. We can still love each other and trust that God's Divine diversity allows for many truths, like the inimitable snowflake that never gets repeated twice. The truth of the heart is as diverse as the snowflake.

On Joy and Delight

One of the many places where practical mysticism can have a profound impact is on the role of parenting. I often wish that every child came with a "How To" manual, but unfortunately we are usually left to our own history or we have to make things up as we go. In this regard, the patterns and ideas about parenting that have been passed down through the generations are staggering. For example, in our society most people believe that one of the many roles of a good parent is to teach their children to succeed. However, one of the hardest and greatest accomplishment of a parent is to teach their children how to fall and how to get back up afterwards. Falling is not the enemy—giving up is. We face a difficult trend in western society that focuses entirely on succeeding, winning, achieving, and very little on personal fulfillment, or development of perseverance and character. It has been said that happiness does not come from getting what you want, but from wanting what you have. We rarely are taught these ideas or instill them in our children. Yet life is really just a series of failures from which we either get back up and learn how to be different, or decide to give up. Every situation has built within it the teaching that comes from working it out. In certain Asian countries, children are applauded and encouraged as they are doing the work toward the goal. When they arrive at the goal, there is silence. The inherent teaching is that the goal is truly not what is important or the source of happiness, but instead the walking of the path.

How much of our lives do we spend doing things that we truly do not want to be doing because we think it will bring us happiness or success? Perhaps we should think again. Or perhaps we should consider redefining what success and failure really mean. For example, if success means taking the lesson in every event, then we are much more likely to succeed than if it means meeting some standard that we or someone else has arbitrarily set. Rockefeller went bankrupt several times before he became a millionaire. Does this mean he was a failure or was this part of his success? Maybe failure is not what we think it is. We must find new ways to look at the world and ourselves that allow us to have all of our experiences without categorizing them as success or failure, right or wrong. Instead, we must see and appreciate the learning.

Our world is focused on eliciting approval from others, rather than ourselves. This comes from the age-old parenting dynamic of showering our little ones with our approval at a job well done. But too often this fosters a focus on what others value rather than ourselves.

Recently I have begun to watch my sister with her little ones. When they come to her with one of their treasures, she asks them what they think about their picture or their grade or their accomplishment. She returns them to themselves and then she responds. She showers them with love and approval for a job well-done or for persevering or for behaving in a compassionate or thoughtful manner. But always she asks them what they think or feel first. In this way, they learn what makes them happy, not just their mom or their world. This is a skill we all need more of if we are to truly have joy in our lives.

Practical mysticism is about doing what makes you happy and what brings delight to your heart. This is not to be confused with a short-term lower-self impulse to escape the very real difficulties of life. But too often we do what a good person is "supposed" to do, believing that God will love us more. In reality, we are just fulfilling someone else's idea of what a "good person" is, and once again, giving away our own authority. This is true whether we are responding to a boss, a parent, a child, a spiritual teacher, a therapist or CNN. Somehow we have learned that other people know what is good for us, even more than we know ourselves. Joy and delight are qualities of the soul. Joy and delight are aspects of the Divine. When we fail to identify what brings us joy, or if we suppress our joy because we think it is not spiritual, we lose the opportunity for happiness.

If we are here to appreciate and bring Divine Presence into this world, what greater way can there be than to bring a bit more joy and delight to the people around us? This is not the same as disrespectful and imbalanced giddiness, which actually comes from not being grounded in the world. Joy and delight mark the Presence of the Shekhina, the Kowthar, the Divine Waterfall of God in the physical body. Not outside of it, but in it. Our bodies are here with us, here as a vessel for the soul. They were designed by the Divine One to give us pleasure and bring us joy. The joy of seeing our little children frolicking in the yard, the delight of a beautiful painting, the enjoyment of exquisite music, all require the physical senses of the body. These are not the same as lower-self or base personality tendencies toward instant gratification, which may be at the expense of others. But all too often, those on the spiritual path tend to disown the very ability to appreciate the beauty of the world and the physical body, and to squelch the joy of the heart because it is seen as "unspiritual." Why would we have been given the flowers and the birds, and lovemaking, and the symphony and all the innate individual talents, and the ability to create, if they were not to be enjoyed?

This brings up the question of how we might know the difference between the joy of the soul and an addictive high. How do we know if we are feeding a lower-self impulse or delighting in the Divine creation? This is a difficult question to answer and there is no simple recipe. But a few overriding themes can be of assistance. The first is to ask if this uplifts the people around us, our partners and family members. Does this action increase their joy? Or does it hurt them in some way? A second is to listen to the Voice of Truth in the heart. The heart never lies. When the Voice of Truth is in delight, when there is a huge "yes" to laughter and lightness and to not take ourselves too seriously, then we know we are headed in the right direction. True joy brings delight and joy to others as well, while an addictive high shuts down the hearts of those around us. True joy is self-perpetuating. It rings through eternity in the heart. Addiction ends in pain and suffering after the initial high is gone.

They say that God is in the details.

So stop. Right now. Wherever you are. Feel the air on your skin. Listen to the sounds of life around you. Look around at all the beautiful things and people in your environment just for a moment. Can you feel the exquisite delight in that? This is the gift of the true spiritual masters. They are present in every moment, which is why they are usually capable of amazing joy at the drop of a hat. They are present in every moment, and are not mentally caught up in the past or in the future. The great masters remain in the present moment.

Most often if we stop in any given moment and just look around, we will see that there is absolutely nothing terrible with right now, that in fact the details around us can bring us joy and pleasure. It is only the worry about other times, other places, other people, other situations, that takes us away from the pleasure of this moment. These God-given qualities of enjoyment of life, though sometimes misused for the purposes of the lower self, are too often judged as bad, unholy, unspiritual or trivial. Yet these are the very qualities that allow us to get up after a perceived failure, to enjoy the moment despite the difficulties, to be able to remain hopeful when everyone around us is not. Somberness has its place. But it is not the only quality of God. We truly need to laugh more and love more, and let ourselves fall on our faces more and get up more, and find that we have learned, and it is all really not as terrible as we had thought. When we can laugh, we can survive failing and we can wake up the next morning and start again.

My first spiritual teacher was my dad. I remember very well the day he taught me about all of this. We were in an airport traveling with the family. Our flight was delayed, there was great confusion, it was hot, and everyone was cranky. Except for him. He sat down in a cramped seat with his cup of coffee and looked around. I asked him what we should do. He said, "Look around. Look at how entertaining the world is." I looked. All I could see was a bunch of cranky, pushy travelers moaning about the delay. And there was my Papa, enjoying the heck out of the moment, letting himself be entertained rather than infuriated. I sat down next to him.

Every once in a while, no matter how difficult, chaotic or painful the circumstance, we should take a moment to just sit down and look at the amazingness of the moment.

Maybe then we will find that success and failure are not what we think, and that greater joy is what a successful life is really all about.

Light
Will someday split you open
Even if your life is now a cage,

For the Divine seed, the crown of destiny,
Is hidden and sown on ancient soil, a fertile plain
You hold the title to.

Love will surely bust you wide open
Into an unfettered, blooming new galaxy,

Even if your mind is now
A spoiled mule.
A life-giving radiance will come,
The Friend's gratuity will come.

O look again within yourself,
For you were once the elegant host
To all the marvels of creation.

From a sacred place in your body
A bow rises each night
And shoots your soul into God.

Behold the Beautiful Drunk Singing One
From the lunar vantage point of love.

He is conducting the affairs
Of the whole universe while throwing wild parties
In a treehouse—on a limb
In your heart.

— Hafiz
The Subject Tonight Is Love
translated by Daniel Ladinsky

The Art of Not Being Offended

There is an ancient and well-kept secret to happiness which the Great Ones have known for centuries. They rarely talk about it, but they use it all the time, and it is fundamental to good mental health. This secret is called The Fine Art of Not Being Offended. In order to truly be a master of this art, one must be able to see that every statement, action and reaction of another human being is the sum result of their total life experience to date. In other words, the majority of people in our world say and do what they do from their own set of fears, conclusions, defenses and attempts to survive. Most of it, even when aimed directly at us, has nothing to do with us. Usually, it has more to do with all the other times, and in particular the first few times, that this person experienced a similar situation, usually when they were young. Yes, this is psychodynamic. But psychodynamics are what make the world go around. An individual who wishes to live successfully in the world as a spiritual person really needs to understand that psychology is as spiritual as prayer. In fact, the word psychology literally means the study of the soul.

All of that said, almost nothing is personal. Even with our closest loved ones, our beloved partners, our children and our friends. We are all swimming in the projections and filters of each other's life experiences and often we are just the stand-ins, the chess pieces of life to which our loved ones have their own built-in reactions. This is not to dehumanize life or take away the intimacy from our relationships, but mainly for us to know that almost every time we get offended, we are actually just in a misunderstanding. A true embodiment of this idea actually allows for more intimacy and less suffering throughout all of our relationships.

When we know that we are just the one who happens to be standing in the right place at the right psychodynamic time for someone to say or do what they are doing—we don't have to take life personally. If it weren't us, it would likely be someone else. This frees us to be a little more detached from the reactions of people around us. How often do we react to a statement of another by being offended rather than seeing that the other might actually be hurting? In fact, every time we get offended, it is actually an opportunity to extend kindness to one who may be suffering—even if they themselves do not appear that way on the surface. All anger, all acting out, all harshness, all criticism, is in truth a form of suffering. When we provide no Velcro for it to stick, something changes in the world. We do not even have to say a thing. In fact, it is usually better not to say a thing. People who are suffering on the inside, but not showing it on the outside, are usually not keen on someone pointing out to them that they are suffering. We do not have to be our loved one's therapist. We need only understand the situation and move on. In the least, we ourselves experience less suffering and at best, we have a chance to make the world a better place.

This is also not to be confused with allowing ourselves to be hurt, neglected or taken advantage of. True compassion does not allow harm to ourselves either. But when we know that nothing is personal, a magical thing happens. Many of the seeming abusers of the world start to leave our lives. Once we are conscious, so-called abuse can only happen if we believe what the other is saying. When we know nothing is personal, we also do not end up feeling abused. We can say, "Thank you for sharing," and move on. We are not hooked by what another does or says, since we know it is not about us. When we know that our inherent worth is not determined by what another says, does or believes, we can take the world a little less seriously. And if necessary, we can just walk away without creating more misery for ourselves or having to convince the other person that we are good and worthy people.

Another great challenge of our world is to live a life of contentment regardless of what other people do, say, think or believe. The fine art of not being offended is one of the many skills for being a practical mystic. Though it may take a lifetime of practice, it is truly one of the best kept secrets for living a happy life.

Mea Culpa

I have a theory about guilt I would like to share with you. The theory is this: guilt is not an innate human emotion. It is not a primal emotion like fear or love or anger. It is a learned response that is inbred by people who, usually unconsciously and usually well-intended, are trying to get us to do what they think we should do.

Parents are famous for this. But they are not alone. Bosses, friends, authority figures of any kind do this. And don't think that even we ourselves are off the hook. We all do it. We have learned from the masters. We have learned that if we can make someone feel guilty enough, we can get them to do what we want them to do.

I first thought about this years ago when a dear friend, who I will call Sarah, was telling me about her difficulties with her family. The story was a familiar one, the family believing surely that Grandma would not be on the earth much longer. (Ironically, not only did this woman live many more years, but she remained a bitter, angry, cold and critical woman throughout her life, bless her soul.) Unfortunately, Sarah's family constantly insisted that she do the "right thing" by visiting this miserable old woman on a regular basis, even though it meant many afternoons of misery. Her grandmother had never once given my dear friend an ounce of love and kindness, never mind the usual grandmother-type things that most of us are blessed to receive. Instead, for most of her life she had been subjected to her grandmother's rejection and criticism, despite repeated efforts to extend herself. And while I am all for visiting old relatives and sick people, I am not for self-abuse. In that conversation, it seemed that Sarah's family was trying to get her to do this so that THEY wouldn't have to. Like a lightning bolt, the insight struck us both at the same time. Their infliction of guilt was being used to control her. That afternoon, as Sarah spoke about this situation, she remembered all the guilt-induced behavior of her life—all the obligatory visits, phone calls and volunteering—every idea that had been given to her about what a "good person" does in the world. She awoke to how much of her life she had spent doing things she really did not want to be doing. She awoke to the fact that her family was in their own cycle of guilt, and guilt had driven the whole system. And in that moment she was freed. While she continues to visit this unhappy old woman, she goes when she wants, when she can, and with a different intention. She goes, not out of obligation or a false sense of responsibility, but in an act of loving kindness. She goes without expecting anything in return, allowing for the tragic unhappiness of this old woman, and finally just accepting her in her humanity and letting go of trying to elicit approval. And Sarah's family has stopped with the guilt trips.

As I began to ponder this, I realized that every time I had done something out of guilt, I had also ended up having a resentment, or somehow being distanced from the very people I loved, but to whom I felt obligated. I held an internal anger that kept me closed to that person in a different way. Although I did the "right thing," I resented it the whole time and I resented the person who had manipulated me into doing it to begin with. Suddenly, being a good person was not what I thought it was. Suddenly I realized that guilt-driven behavior actually destroyed relationships rather than built them, since underneath the surface, the heart connection was lost.

Yet none of this should be confused with having a conscience. Conscience is an innate quality. We all know when we are doing something hurtful to another. We all know when the moment arrives to support a friend or offer help to a loved one. But this is something that arises from within. There is no guilt attached to it. We just do it. We do it because we want to do it or because it is the right thing in the moment and we feel an internal call to offer ourselves. It is rooted in love, not guilt.

Unfortunately, too often we do something out of obligation. What is obligation really, other than something we do because we think we should, and then ultimately we end up feeling trapped from it in the end? How much of our lives do we spend doing things we don't even want to be doing? Who decides what the right thing is for us? Is it society, or our spouses, or our parents, or our religion? None of those sources are connected to the internal conscience and knowledge of who we are as individuals. Only we ourselves can ever really know what is right for us. If we embark on that journey of self-awareness, guilt only presents itself when some external other, possibly even from decades earlier in our life, wants us to do something else.

In the end, if we are to be ethical people in the world, guilt becomes useless. It creates resentment, self-hatred and frustration. It breaks relationships from behind the scenes and works like a silent virus until one day the pressure blows and we push away the very person we are trying to please. Or we lose our own sense of well-being or physical health. If we truly want good, solid, intimate relationships, we will look for the places where another is manipulating us, usually unconsciously, to do what they want us to do. We will see it and call it by name. Then, without anger, we will listen to our conscience instead of our guilt. In this manner choice is returned. People rarely do this to us intentionally, and we rarely do this to others intentionally. We are just doing what we have learned over eons of time, probably handed down for generations since the day a cavemen discovered 10,000 years ago that it worked! A fine line exists between understanding what is happening and being upset with the people who are doing it. Once they see the dynamic, most people do not want to continue in this way anyhow. Most are not intentionally trying to hurt or manipulate us. They are just trying to get their own needs met in the only way they know. But that does not mean we have to keep the system going.

Perhaps we can use guilt as a warning sign that someone somewhere is trying to manipulate us, even if it is the primal voice of a parent imprinted decades ago. Conscience, on the other hand, knows what is right. Conscience is aligned with right action because it is connected to our own inner heart. Conscience is seated in our soul, while guilt is connected to the wishes or beliefs of another person. They are two very different things.

As practical mystics, we must begin to discern the difference between guilt and conscience. When we start to use other motivators, the nature of our universe begins to change and all of what we do is rooted in choice rather than obligation. And then, our world starts to shift to include relationships with people we want to be with, rather than people we have to be with, and to include acts of loving kindness based on the true need of the moment. To allow this is to truly give with joy and delight. The shift is utterly internal, in one moment of awareness. In one moment we can free ourselves. And when we do, the whole universe changes.

I want to engage with life completely, and then find God in every moment.

— *Rabbi Rolando Matalon*
Rabbinic Leader, Bnai Jeshurun Congregation
New York, New York

Emotional Alchemy

Hidden within every negative feeling is the gem of its opposite. As human beings we tend to do everything possible to avoid feeling bad, and legitimately so. Why on earth would we want to continue to suffer? When pain occurs, we resist, we struggle, we act out, we defy, we avoid, we grieve—all because we think we shouldn't feel this way.

Yet it is the feeling itself which has the information for us about how to feel better. A practical mystic knows this. A practical mystic knows that a seemingly illogical action is required in response to negative feelings—the action of leaning into the discomfort. This change in direction is a difficult one, and one which seems counterintuitive. Why would we ever want to lean into something that hurts so much or feels so bad? Unfortunately, much of our suffering is from the resistance to the reality of the moment. Stress is exactly that—resistance, fighting or struggling with the overload of the current circumstance. But in one of the unusual paradoxes of emotional health, by merely allowing a feeling, by giving it space in our body, mind and soul, we are gently brought to the distant shore of its opposite, to the revelation of what is hidden within. If alchemy is about transforming something of less value into something of greater value, this is truly emotional alchemy.

The physical and emotional worlds are worlds of duality. This means that everything can have a positive or negative use. A knife can be used to inflict harm or to perform life-saving surgery. The essential element is intent. So it is with the emotional world as well. Our challenge is to discover the other side of the negative feeling. This is not done by "thinking positively," which actually covers over and creates more content for the unconscious mind. It is done by allowing the emotion to be present long enough for its opposite to be revealed. It is done by asking what the gem is in grief, what the hidden treasure is in pain.

All fear can be transformed into excitement. All neglect can be transformed into freedom, all anger transformed into choice and right action. Not until we develop the ability to bear the feelings in their raw state first, not by dumping them on others but by tolerating them within ourselves, can we then carry what we wish to avoid. When we do this, we slowly develop emotional muscles. We make ourselves big enough to bear the emotion and get to the other side more quickly. If we do not, avoidance and postponement only prolong the suffering. As they say in the twelve step programs, the only way out is through. Isn't it ironic that we are so afraid of leaning into the discomfort because we think it will be prolonged, or that we will be wallowing in it? Yet in reality, it is avoidance that prolongs the discomfort. Who would have thought this? It does defy all reason.

You might ask, "How does this happen?" I have no answer to this other than it is one of the great mysteries of the universe and how it happens can only be discovered in the doing. You might ask, "How do I know the difference between wallowing in negativity and carrying a negative emotion to make space for it in my being?" While there is no easy answer to this either, we have some clues. Wallowing is actually a form of avoidance. It is an indulgence in self-pity based on a belief that something should not be happening for some reason. It is a very subtle and tricky form of resistance. But it is resistance, coming from a place deep down inside that believes an injustice has been done and it should not have happened. In this way, wallowing is what some have called "secondary pain," an easier pain to bear than the pain of the real thing. Secondary pain is a brilliant way to avoid the real thing and we humans have remarkable ways of creating it. When we discover our tricks, we are again challenged not to engage in self-retribution, but to be willing to just shift our attention and find a place to hold the real thing we have actually been avoiding.

It is only logical that as human beings, we all want to be happy. We want to avoid discomfort and suffering. We label certain feelings as bad and others as more desirable. But this belief becomes like emotional quicksand. The harder we struggle, the deeper it gets. Resistance makes it worse. Yet few tools are given to us other than criticism, self-hatred, avoidance or emotional tirades. This is another great quandary of being human. Where is the manual for dealing with emotions in a healthy way? Where are the classes for being a great parent? How are we supposed to learn these things without so much suffering? Our parents are only doing what they were taught by people who were doing what they were taught. Perhaps someday we will see free parenting skills classes and emotional skills classes as part of every school curriculum. Until then, we must learn on our own and teach

each other. Practical mystics do this as well. But they teach by invitation only and never impose their knowledge onto someone except by request.

The world is filled with fixers, people who want to make everything right. Though the intention is a beautiful one—to alleviate suffering—fixing only cripples people. It is like going to college for someone, taking all the classes and then presenting them with a degree. They learn nothing. Most fixing is born out of the incapacity to bear the suffering of another. A practical mystic knows they must learn to bear the suffering of others as well as their own. Not because they are masochistic or because suffering should continue, but because within all suffering is a gem of knowledge. We must find the teachings of our suffering if we are to create a different world. We must allow our children and our loved ones to learn their lessons without doing it for them or removing the pain temporarily because we cannot bear it. That is ultimately a selfish act. The selfless alternative is to teach the skills we speak about and become a model in the world by doing this ourselves. While it is essential to bear the struggles of another, this does not mean we abandon our loved ones. When it is their time in the desert, we can hold their hand, we can stand by their side and be completely with them. We can be a beloved to them, we can give support and encouragement and gentle, soothing words of the heart, but they must walk out on their own power. While this may seem initially illogical, the proof is in the doing. In the end, we all must walk out of our own desert by bearing our own pain and finding the distant shore. Ideally, we will have the privilege of being surrounded by loving companions.

A practical mystic is ultimately interested in what works in the world. Emotional alchemy is one such paradigm. Logic states we should avoid discomfort at all costs, yet we are asked to do the unthinkable and bear the unbearable. We are asked to see the value in negative feelings. In the carrying of our suffering in a true way, we discover its hidden gift that could not possibly be known in any other way. We are able to redeem the light, not only in what is beautiful, but in what is not so beautiful as well. Therein lies the challenge of humanity. The work of life is to be in our imperfection and be alright with it. In the richness of that acceptance, emotions are transformed and life in all its ups and downs can find a place to rest.

If there are secrets to happiness, one of them is this. It is not in the elimination of all that is bad or unhealed, but in developing the capacity to bear those parts and find the beauty in them in the process. This is emotional alchemy at its best.

Do We Really Create Our Own Reality?

For most of my life, I have worked with people struggling with chronic illness, emotional discomfort and relationship difficulties. Over the course of this time, the consciousness movement has presented some interesting theories about the cause of suffering. Many of the current teachings propose that the mind and distorted beliefs are the source of most illness and that in fact we "create" our own illnesses by our thinking.

I beg to differ. Unfortunately, this philosophy itself can contribute to even more guilt and suffering by imposing an additional measure of self-blame and self-hatred. This is not the direction we want to take. While I do believe that most illness has a mental and emotional root, often that root is preverbal, primal, and beyond the reach of the everyday conscious mind. The path to finding that root involves courageous work with the unconscious and is often a very complex path to wellness. Before many people even arrive at the starting point, they misunderstand the idea of "creating your own reality" and use it as another source of guilt and self-hatred. Perhaps there is a different way to start the path to well-being. Perhaps it is a matter of asking a different question. Rather than asking, "What am I doing wrong?" or "How did I create this?" we might rather ask, "What is this issue bringing into my life?" There is a great and profound difference between blaming ourselves and asking what a situation is here to bring us, yet this subtle difference is rarely stressed. Too often, a loving, kind-hearted person has sunk into self-hatred and greater suffering by believing they have done something "wrong" to bring about their illness. The tragedy here is that the result is greater suffering, not relief.

We are here on this earth to learn. We are given many avenues for this learning to take place. One of them is through the body. The body is the miraculous learning ground for the soul.

For those of us who believe in a Divine Intelligence, this is even more profound, since every great tradition in the world teaches a variation of the following: "God gives to whom S/He wills and God takes away from Whom S/He wills." The implication here is that we, in our humble humanity, can never presume to know why we are given certain challenges. The minute we do, we are playing God.

Therefore, the best we can do is ask what reason this challenge has been given to us. Perhaps it is merely to keep the scales of humanity balanced. For example, isn't it amazing that many great human beings with an exceptional gift have been given an equally difficult challenge, impairment or burden? And it seems the greater the gift, the greater the cross to bear in some other way. Beethoven was deaf. Roosevelt was crippled. Mick Jagger has bad hair.

The point is that no human being is exempt from suffering and the scales are always balanced. To spend our lives fighting what we have been given because we believe it is "bad," (or worse, that we are bad!) is a waste of our time and energy. Maybe the solution lies in looking elsewhere, possibly even a radically different philosophy. What if we were to turn and embrace every single thing that we hate about ourselves and our lives? What if we were to make peace with our cross to bear rather than try to change our belief system so it will go away? There is a secret here in understanding right use of will. We return once again to the philosophy and question of what healing really is. Perhaps healing is the relief of suffering rather than the relief of symptoms. What if every symptom, challenge, difficulty and disease remained exactly as it was but we stopped hating ourselves for having it, stopped questioning what we were doing "wrong," and therefore the suffering of the struggle were ended? Most of us believe that if we are struggling, it means we care. Can we stop struggling and still care? Can we stop worrying and still know we are concerned about those we love?

Many years ago, I was suffering deeply from serious and life-threatening chronic illness. I had been to every traditional and non-traditional specialist I knew, from energetic healers to Columbia Presbyterian specialists. One morning I woke up and decided I was going to stop running around spending all of my time and money trying to "fix" what was "wrong" with me. I decided to arrange my life to accommodate the fact that I was always going to have this disease, I was always going to be uncomfortable to some degree and I was going to live with it. I decreased my work hours, I kept my environment impeccably clean, I tried to get enough rest and eat the right things. I adjusted my life to accommodate this "terrible" illness. The change was very slow, but subtle and profound. It was like watching the grass grow. One day I realized that although I was still often uncomfortable, I wasn't suffering. I wasn't hating myself and I wasn't depressed. I was happy and having a reasonably functional life. To this day I do not do everything that "normal" people do. But I do not suffer. (And truly, what is normal anyway? Isn't it usually just other people's outsides being compared to our own insides?) I accommodate my life—end of story.

Maybe some day I'll find the deep-seated reason for this condition, but frankly I was born with it and perhaps it's just plain genetics. Sometimes a cigar is just a cigar, and sometimes illness is just plain what you got from your ancestors. And sometimes what you got from your ancestors is not always a bad thing. Illness results in a very subtle sensitivity in the world that allows for intuitive understanding at a very deep level. I don't know if I healed today if I would lose my high sense perception, but I do know that the physical state I was born into provides me with tremendous sensitivity to the subtle workings of the world. Do I need this illness? Maybe, maybe not. I suspect there is a primal wound that happened in infancy which I have not yet been able to uncover. Maybe some day I will get to it. But in the meantime, why suffer? There is enough struggle in the world already. Believe it or not, we can be happy in spite of and including the fact that we have not healed every imperfection and physical/emotional/spiritual difficulty—by allowing them to be what they are while they are still around. This does not mean that we don't care or we don't try to improve the conditions of our lives. We must continue to seek every possible means of help and to follow up on every option for healing. We must not confuse acceptance with resignation or despair. In fact, despair is about NOT accepting what is. Making a place for the less-than-wonderful things in our lives does not mean we give up. It just means we don' have to suffer while we are still learning.

In many parts of the world water is scarce and precious.
People sometimes have to walk a great distance
Then carry heavy jugs upon their heads.
Because of our wisdom, we will travel far for love.
All movement is a sign of Thirst.
Most speaking really says, "I am hungry to know you."
Every desire of your body is holy;
Every desire of your body is Holy.
Dear one, why wait until you are dying
To discover that divine truth?

— Hafiz
The Subject Tonight Is Love
Translated by Daniel Ladinsky

Working With the Shadow

Someone once said that the fast track to consciousness is to see every judgement as a disowned part of the self that needs to be reclaimed. In other words, judgement is our friend. The judgements we have of others are the very things that we abhor within ourselves and they point to where our own self-hatred and inner critic poison our psyche. Many of the great mystical traditions teach that everything is energy, and energy in itself is not good or bad. But the use of an energy in a negative way is usually a protective attempt of a very vulnerable side of ourselves designed to keep us safe. Thus a judgement is an attempt to keep ourselves safe.

This is where the spiritual path can sometimes cause difficulties. Many spiritual traditions speak about purification, a word which implies the elimination of something "bad." As long as there is a split between good and bad, right and wrong, there is a need to "cut out" the "bad" parts. The ultimate result of this can only be suppression and further pain. We end up avoiding the undercurrents of our vulnerabilities and the power sides which have been created to protect them.

There is no possible way that the psyche can "eliminate" a "bad" thought, action or behavior, but can only redirect it to a more useful service. And this can only be done after there has been an understanding of how initially the behavior was created to help us, even if it now seems twisted and damaging. Every dysfunctional behavior is, in actuality, a survival tool that worked at some point in our lives, even if it was twenty years ago. The problem is that we continue to behave as if the danger in our environment still exists. Until a judged or distorted behavior is given a new job description, its only choice is to go underground and hide, or to come out in very destructive ways that are not within our conscious control. These unconscious protector energies are the source of our deepest pain and suffering.

We tend to project our unconscious onto the outside or onto our relationships, since we cannot bear the thought that this could be something that exists in ourselves, and the cosmic judo of the unconscious finds ingenious ways to express the quality that is not "allowed" by the conscious mind.

The creative alternative is to do our own shadow work by looking at and exploring the darker, less pleasant sides of our personality. In this regard, I have discovered that misunderstandings abound about shadow work, so I would like to address a few of them.

The first is the misunderstanding that a healer or spiritual teacher or therapist can take away the unconscious dynamic without any work or consciousness on the part of the individual. While it is true that a pattern can be temporarily moved, suppressed or changed, other than a few rare exceptions, long-term transformation can only occur with awareness of our actions and the subtle forces behind them. We then have the option to be different. A second misunderstanding is that a spiritual practice can bypass the need for shadow work.

Unfortunately, neither of these are true. In fact, if we do not work on bringing the unconscious into our awareness, then the path of enlightenment will only add more charge to the shadow.

When we open to the higher transpersonal energies without having explored our instinctual or protector energies, the potential for difficulties is great. With every step into awakening, we must go to the other side and explore the shadow aspect that would use even this to its own advantage. Without having embraced both, without being able to contain both the dark and the light of our own inner landscape, we will end up using even spiritual or personal growth to feed our shadow. The alternative is to truly understand how to live in this world where the darkness and the light live so close together. God made everything, both the darkness and the light. The awareness of how to manage both the light and the dark can be life-changing. This is not to say that we should become or act out our shadow side. In fact, we end up acting out our shadow side when we have not explored it, entered into it, and worked with it in its raw state. As spiritual beings, we have a tendency to want to purify something away before we truly know what it is and this can never be a long-term solution. But the nature of the unconscious is that it is unconscious. If we knew what was there, we would work with it.

Since by its nature, we cannot inherently be conscious of the unconscious, our judgements are the doorway to our shadow. Equally so are our dreams, daydreams, fantasies and all of our suffering. They each point to the unconscious aspects in ourselves that are calling to be understood. We must then give them a place inside of us, not necessarily to be acted upon.

Therefore, if you are interested in the fast track to well-being and consciousness, explore your judgements and find the hidden value of their meaning within your own life. Every quality has a purpose. Every energy has a reason for being, even if it has been highly distorted from its original intent. It came to us for a reason and served us in some way even if it is now outdated and unnecessary. Somewhere along the way it saved us from something worse—possibly even saved our life— and we must honor that fact.

The ancient religious concept that the body is evil and something to be escaped, or the personality is something to be overcome has no place in practical mysticism. For as long as we are alive in this world, we will always need both a body and a personality. The dual nature of these means that there will always be a new challenge, no matter how enlightened we may become. And mastering the energetics of our inner life is a means of finding happiness regardless of what is happening around us.

In addition, pretending that we are not in judgement is in fact a shadow in itself. Judgement is a reality of life here on this earth. We need it in order to survive. Sometimes it goes too far. But true awareness, true consciousness, true enlightenment, and the quality of true Divine love is not necessarily about being nice all the time. It is not about appearing peaceful, but rather it is about being truthful—truthful with ourselves about exactly where we are and truthful with others about who we are.

When we are at our most vulnerable, when we are at the deepest truth within the shadow self, is paradoxically when we are closest to God. Truth creates proximity to the Divine, even when the truth is something we despise or something we believe we should not be feeling after all the work we have done. By being in truth, we become aligned with the deeper aspects of who we are and integration occurs. Thus, we become more of who we really are and find ourselves at the foot of the Divine Throne as a result. As it has been said by my beloved teacher Jason Shulman, "God does not want my perfection, but only my honesty."

In this regard, every judgement becomes an opportunity to become more aware in our relationship with ourselves, our loved ones and ultimately with the Divine.

One does not become enlightened by imagining figures of light,
but by making the darkness conscious.

— Carl Jung

SECTION III: SEPTEMBER 11

Transformation and the Sublime

On September 11, 2001, our world changed forever. Even after the dust has literally settled, the lessons continue. This event was an archetypal trauma, a community experience which taught us, one more time, how to connect, how to grieve, how to deal with sudden and profound loss…not just out of a textbook, but from a living reality. It is my wish that we not forget these lessons. They apply to us every day. Every day we are faced with loss, sudden change, unexpected intrusions into our life. Though, God-willing, they are usually on a smaller scale, they are still very real to each of us as they happen. As spiritual people, we are often called to find the beauty in the moment, or to cherish what we have rather than wish for what we do not have. September 11 brought this very close to home. It is this lesson that I hope we will never forget. While I often heard many people state that they had seen enough, read enough, and were tired of the images of 9/11, I never once experienced that. Rather, I was pulled to the television and the bookstore. I had a sense that nothing like this would ever happen again in my lifetime and I wanted to understand it as deeply as possible.

The photography of Joel Meyerowitz, the official photographer of Ground Zero, had particular impact (*see Resources List at back of book for more information about his work*). His capacity to capture in still image the emotion, tone and quality of this event is profound. In an interview on NPR, I heard him speak about his definition of the sublime, the capacity to see the exquisite beauty and the horror at the same time, even amidst devastating tragedy. His work speaks to the very idea of holding two opposing things in one place, even in image and form. It is the very nature of the sublime that carries my attention to 9/11 even to this day. We have hardly begun to draw out the lessons of this magnanimous event. The challenge is to do so without reliving nightmares and creating victimization in place of empowerment.

To this end—of remembering the awesomeness and culling out the relevant gems for our lives even now—I include here the writings, articles and diary of correspondence that occurred in the days immediately following 9/11. Perhaps there is relevancy to our daily life, even now.

WEDNESDAY, SEPTEMBER 12 9:33 AM

Beloved Friends:

I am drawn to share some thoughts with you about this devastating tragedy as the implications of it begin to sink in...

The grief appears in unusual and unexpected ways. As we hear that the last person we have been concerned about is well, or at least as well as it can be in this circumstance, I realize that this is a community trauma. Regardless of whether or not people have beloveds involved in the actual terror act, the act has been perpetrated on all of us who live here.

I drive down Route 17 to my New Jersey office on this clear and sunny day. In these conditions we always see the New York skyline. Today there is a gaping hole where the World Trade Center previously stood. It feels as if a universal body part has been amputated.

I try to call my family in Massachusetts, but because the South Tower of the Trade Center was the transmitter for so many modes of communication, it takes me hours to get through. I am acutely aware of how much we have come to rely on the telecommunications system of the day. Only my cell phone works—even now. The land lines are still down. I realize that I will probably never again leave my house without a cell phone.

Throughout the past 24 hours I have received a flood of phone calls from friends in Israel—people who have been trying for hours to get through. I am struck by how the Israeli people have lived with this kind of thing for years. They are the first to offer help and support. One dear friend stayed up through the night until 5 AM waiting to get through just to be sure we are OK.

I received an e-mail from a friend in Boston about a business opportunity. No acknowledgement of anything that has happened. I realize that what we see on TV has become so remote that unless we are on ground zero we do not apply it to ourselves.

Another friend calls from downtown, describing it like a nuclear winter. My brother in-law, who worked in the building across the street from the Twin Towers, remained to help a friend in distress and then walked all the way up town after watching the building come down in front of his very eyes. He walks to my sister-in-law's house, cleans off her bike and rides for hours to get home in Long Island. When he gets home he throws his clothes in the trash because they are so dust-laden, and calls to ask what is the best way to get asbestos out of your lungs.

Another old friend who worked in Building 7 calls. He just watched the building collapse on CNN and every personal treasure, photos from his trips around the world, his address books with all the numbers, appointments, personal info, favorite CD's, his financial statements, are annihilated in one moment. The office where he worked yesterday no longer exists on this earth. He has no idea when he will return to work or what is happening. He has no one to call, since every work-related number he had went to that building. He waits at home for a call from someone who might have information about his office, his future, his paycheck and his career.

Most of my clients call today to cancel, saying they cannot imagine talking about their own lives in light of this tragedy. I understand. And the paradox is that life must go on. We MUST remain involved in our petty lives, if only to ground us in the ability to carry on.

How can someone across the river in New Jersey be so impacted? I can only say that the fabric of our lives has been torn at the root at the levels of culture and society. We must not minimize this trauma and we must get up and carry on at the same time. Life will never be the same. We have been violated at the core of our being on a psychic, energetic, spiritual and most likely financial level.

In spite of it all, the goodness of humanity has shown itself repeatedly through these days. These events only serve to bring out the best of who we are. I hope we will see that aspect along with the tragedy. Please join us if you can at sunset for the next two nights as we pray for those victims who have unexpectedly been taken from this earth and those who have been left behind.

And may God shed Her mercy on each and every one of us.

SUNDAY, SEPTEMBER 16

Beloved Friends:

Today is the day before the beginning of the Jewish New Year, a time specifically set aside for redemption and forgiveness. As much as I speak about, teach and believe in the ideas of forgiveness and personal responsibility, this is a time when it takes a Herculean effort of the soul to think along such lines. I want to share with you a few recent experiences.

I have been in the city quite a bit in an effort to contribute in some small way. The hardest part for me has been the drives up and down the West Side highway, when on several occasions I have seen the police escort of dump trucks filled with debris and most likely parts or possessions of someone who once worked in the buildings. I have to pull over every time. I wonder where they are going. I wonder what it must feel like to be driving those trucks. I cannot stop thinking how similar this is to the Holocaust. I cannot but worry that precious human remains might be dumped in some back lot in New Jersey. I call my synagogue, and they tell me that they have already organized a minyan to go out to the dumping site and pray over the piles. Human beings are amazing.

The paradox of the normal routine of life that has to go on, that MUST go on, interjected with the sudden reality of the situation. As I watched a movie about a story based in Manhattan, I kept praying they would not show the twin towers on the screen. They didn't. But I wonder how I will feel the first time there is an image of the skyline in front of me. The visual impact has been one of the greatest traumas for the local residents, not just in Manhattan, but across the river in New Jersey where almost every family has someone they know or loved who worked in the building. The visual trauma from the other side of the bridge is beyond description.

I realize that the people in New Jersey, Connecticut and Long Island have been as traumatized as New Yorkers, just in a different way. Summit, NJ lost over thirty residents at this point and they are still counting.

I drive up Broadway, where people are going about their business. The deli is open, Starbucks is open. But on the corner is the bomb squad with police in gas masks checking the trash barrels.

I now feel exactly the way I feel every day in Jerusalem. No one goes out without a cell phone. Public trash cans do not exist. An armed guard at every public restaurant. This is no longer Jerusalem I am speaking about, it is New York.

As I walk down the street even now, almost a week later, people seem stunned. The silent look of shock is everywhere, paralyzing. I am torn between concern for this and concern for another phenomena that seems to be happening through the rest of the country…maybe even the world. People wanting so much to get beyond this and on with their lives, that they make up an internal story that covers over the grief, the overwhelming devastation of this event. Anything to get out of the numbing zombie-like effects of this tragedy. If there has ever been a time not to push the river, not to rush the process, not to drown the rose bud with water so that it will bloom faster, this is it.

Our hearts are breaking. May we let them break completely before trying to spackle over the broken parts. There is strength in our brokenness. May we allow it to be so for all of us and for as long as it takes. It is a teaching about the process of grieving and it touches every one of us somehow, in all the places and times of our lives when we have had our own personal 9/11.

Shana Tova to each and every one of you.

WEDNESDAY, SEPTEMBER 19

Beloved Soul Companions:

I have sat down numerous times to try to write a response to the many requests for words about this event. I am still too close to it to feel I have the right words in that regard. I can only share my experiences on a day-to-day basis. But in the midst of it all, I have received an e-mail from my beautiful brother, whose humble soul shines like a light to everyone around him, though he would never say so. He is not a Sufi or a Rabbi or a monk. But he has always been my teacher. I share this with you as an offering of what I would say if I could.

Hi Sis,

Thanks for all your words of wisdom and compassion. My friend Chip shared with me a quote from the Buddha that you might find thought provoking. Buddha said: "What is forgiveness if we cannot forgive the unforgivable? Anyone can forgive the forgivable."

I have also been thinking about the expression, "These are the times that try men's souls..." understanding it fully perhaps for the first time. I certainly think that this event will put our national character to the test, and I hope that we can focus on building a peaceful future, rather than a holy crusade of vengeance.

I still cannot quite believe what has occurred. Given the context of the immediate, vivid images we saw over and over again on TV, this must be the most shocking single event in world history. It is comforting, however, to observe the sense of worldwide community that has arisen in response to this tragedy. I trust that it is this empathy that will see us through this crisis.

Love,

Bob

FRIDAY SEPTEMBER 21, 2001

ON THE NATURE OF TRAUMA AND DIVINE PURPOSE

Reflections on 9/11 Ten Days Later

In our attempts to make sense out of the unexplainable, there is very little for us to fall back on, other than one thing. If God exists, if there is a Divine Intelligence and a higher plan, there MUST be a reason why this can be allowed. If God is a benevolent being, how on earth could such a thing happen?

Possibly this is the ultimate example of the lower serving the higher. Sometimes we need a wake-up call to galvanize our actions as the force of good. Whoever was behind this tragedy was attempting to break our spirits. But the mission has failed. Never in the history of the world has there been such an outpouring of goodness, support, love, caring, donation, self-sacrifice, prayers and gratitude. The veil of safety and security has been pierced in this past week and we have had to create a new form of safety that comes from the bonding through the heart.

Though some may return to their old ways, New York has become a kinder city, while at the same time a tougher one. The paradox of kindness and might have come together here in a way that only God could create. No doubt that trauma is a terrible and tragic thing. We must not sugarcoat it or pretend it does not shake the foundations of our existence. There is not a single person in this part of the world who is not aware that the other has been affected. The first thing we say is, "Are you alright? Is everyone in your family OK? Did you have anyone there?" We know they have experienced their own version of loss. And they have experienced the loss regardless of whether they have known someone directly or not. Anyone living in this area has been deeply and profoundly shaken by this event. It has affected us personally, no matter who we are. We must remember this time. We must remember so that we take the learning and continue, or at least return to, the amazing place we are in right now. We will not tolerate abuse of our good heartedness. But we will also be gentle with each other and know that every single one of us hurts. Our hearts have been broken into pieces. But they have been broken open together. We understand the pain of each other and thereby the pain of humanity. Let us always keep our suffering close enough so that we know that every soul has its own deep pain, but far enough away that we are not immobilized. God is both gentle and mighty. We must use these qualities as a model for living in a new way, for moving past the loss of the world as we knew it on September 11 into a new world that is even better than before. We cannot let evil drag our hearts into fear, darkness, retribution and eternal resentment. We must take that evil and let it strengthen our resolve to be mighty against hatred and gentle with each other.

This is the nature of why trauma and God can exist in the same world. It is now up to us to live differently, to live with compassion and yet live with strength of character that does not allow abuse of our souls. Perhaps we all need a bit more knowledge that sometimes "No" is a Divine word too.

The minute I am disappointed I am encouraged.
When I am ruined, I am healed.
When ruined and brought low to the ground,
Then I speak the low tones of thunder for everyone.

— *Rumi*
The Glance
Translated by Coleman Barks

SECTION IV: SPIRITUAL PATHS AND MYSTICISM

They have no shame, no honor, no fear for what is to come. They are secure, says Love. Their doors are open. No one can harm them.

— Marguerite Porete
The Mirror of Simple Souls
1310

Introduction

This section is designed to provide a cursory look at several mystical paths rooted in the monotheistic traditions, the children of Abraham so to speak. While each of the traditions of Judaism, Christianity and Islam have their own culture and practice, they can all be traced back to one father—the prophet Abraham. The Abrahamic lineage continues today, and perhaps it is by remaining true to the quality of the soul, doing our own shadow work and extending a hand of peace to the rest of the family, that a new world might be created.

You will find in this section an introduction to the mystical traditions of the three monotheistic paths, each followed by an esoteric text. If you are already familiar with a tradition, you may find the esoterica more interesting. If you are unfamiliar with the mystical traditions of Kabbalah, Theosophy and Sufism you may want to read just the introductory piece of each.

A cautionary reminder to those who enjoy esoteric text: more people have walked the path of spiritual glamour than spiritual enlightenment. Always ground what you learn of the unseen world in your daily life or your education will be meaningless. Practical mystics are dedicated to changing the world we live in through action, speech and intention, and usually in small unglamorous ways, one interaction at a time. True esoteric knowledge is usually the fruit of many years of study and best when received through the direct transmission of an honorable teacher. What you read here is just a taste. But if esoterica is your thing, read with gusto. May these texts give up their secrets with ease, insight and relevance to your life.

Snowflakes and the Path of the Soul

It has been snowing here for three days. I am one of those people who loves the snow, as God seems more real to me than ever in Her miraculous transformation of the earth into a gentle, silent winter wonderland. The world and the people in it seem kinder in the snow, and I am reminded of a story I heard about snowflakes from an old and dear friend. Most of us have heard through the years that every snowflake is a unique creation. But my curiosity has always been about why and how it got this way. According to my friend George, this is how it goes....

All snowflakes begin their journey to earth exactly the same way, as a six-sided hexagonal molecule of water. But as they slowly descend, each snowflake bumps into another snowflake hexagon, which attaches to one of its six sides. Sometimes it bumps into a clump of hexagons. As the journey continues, this snowflake may be blown to the east or the west, or sometimes even back upward for a short bit, depending on the wind and the moisture. All of this results in a path that is extremely unique for each snowflake. No two snowflakes follow the same route to the earth and therefore no two snowflakes are exactly the same.

This analogy is very similar to the path of the soul. Each soul descends to earth in a very unique way, sometimes moving west, sometimes moving east, sometimes dropping straight down. The mystics teach that the path of return is the same way. We must follow our original path back to God. Therefore each path is unique and unusual in its own way. No two souls can return in exactly the same way. Each snowflake soul must remember how it got here and call itself back through that route and the spiritual breadcrumbs it left on the way down.

Remembering our route home is, for sure, a challenge. But our clues lie in the preferences, places and people to which we are instinctually drawn. If we force ourselves to be in places that seem popular or "right" but which are not true to our root, we will often experience discomfort, depression, loneliness or some form of unhappiness. This is only because we are not in the place that resonates with our soul, and it is the reason why so many different spiritual paths exist in our world. No one "route" can provide the path of return for all snowflake souls. If we happen to be in a place that seems like the "right" place according to other people, but we are not happy and fulfilled, it is likely that there is another route that is closer to our true makeup. Sometimes it takes many adventures, many false starts, and many attempts at finding our route, until we find the exact place that feels like our true path of return. Sometimes we stay in places far longer than is best for us, trying to convince ourselves that we are in the right place, since everyone around us seems to be happy or getting what they need. These are the times when courageous self-honesty is the most difficult and yet the most important. And if we have found our home, but realize that someone we love is not happy, we must find a place in our heart to honor that their route may not be the same as ours. One route is not higher, better or more worthy than the other. Just different—like the snowflakes. It is hard to imagine what our world would look like if every snowflake were the same.

But it seems even now, as I look out my window at the gentle rain of snowshowers, it is in the very uniqueness of snowflakes that God's beauty and Divine Wisdom is expressed.

Kabbalah and Its Relevance to Modern Life

Kabbalah is the term most often applied to a particular set of mystical teachings within the Jewish tradition. In recent years it has become well-known, not only among Jews, but also among people of other faiths. Many reasons for this exist, but one is that Kabbalah is both rooted in ancient tradition and relevant to the consciousness of our time. It therefore is the ultimate in practical mysticism.

The origins of Kabbalah are surrounded in the usual mystique of every great tradition. But the work of the Kabbalists of Safed in the 1500's brought its essence into outer form and practical spiritual discipline. Kabbalah remains relevant today because it deals with the world of archetypes and root-cause metaphor rather than the outer manifestation. We therefore have a teaching whose emphasis is on the pre-creational cause of both suffering and well being, providing skills to bring about meaningful change and body/mind wellness.

The current controversy in Kabbalistic circles is whether the time has come for the general population to be brought into these teachings. In ages past, the great masters taught that only married Jewish men over forty years old were of the capacity to receive these teachings and use them wisely. But almost 500 years ago, a great and widely renowned Kabbalist, Isaac Luria, retracted that dictum, stating that the time had come for this science to be brought out to the public, and that the world was of sufficient maturity for these teachings to be given to everyone. Though the debate continues, suffice it to say that these are powerful concepts which are vital to the world in which we live, especially in light of continuing tragedies here and around the world. At this point we risk more if we do not study the teachings of the sages (such as Kabbalah or other spiritual disciplines that go beyond the rigidity of traditional religion) than if we prevent their study. The time has come for us all to understand the workings of the unseen world in a way that is practical and that helps make real change in the way we live in the third millennium.

There are a few primary concepts of Kabbalah, concepts that mark places where Kabbalah might be different from other modalities.

The first is the concept of the vessel. The Kabbalists believe, contrary to many healing arts and sciences, that healing cannot be given to or done to or made to happen by the healer. Nothing is ever willfully or intentionally moved, changed, pushed in or pulled out. The will of the healer is considered not only irrelevant but often a hindrance to the healing force. The skill of the Kabbalist lies therefore in a completely different arena than with most energetic and traditional medicine techniques. The skill lies in the complete absence of the self, absence of ideas about healing, and about what should happen. Rather, the skill involves the ability to become a completely empty vessel so that the Divine Intelligence can find its place.

This concept of absence of self to allow the Divine healing (or "tikkun") to emerge is rooted in an ancient teaching about creation, called the tzim tzum. The Kabbalists teach that in the beginning God was all-pervasive and all-encompassing. But for something new to be created, S/He had to withdraw itself back in order to create a space for something "other" to exist. This withdrawal of the Divine Self was called the tzim tzum and was the pre-creational act that allowed for all of existence to be brought into being. The tzim tzum is a profound teaching about relationship. Its model teaches us that we must withdraw ourselves, with our all-encompassing egos and needs, in order to allow another to exist. To be in relationship, we must let go of some of the psychic space that we tend to fill with our own ideas, needs, and wants, and make room for the reality of the other who may be very different. We need to make enough space for an other to exist. The tzim tzum shows us that just by the very nature of pulling back and making enough space, the other is more fulfilled.

Therefore, in Kabbalah we learn more and more how to pull ourselves back, empty the psychic space so that the other can find the Divine Intelligence and healing, the unique tikkun that is needed specifically for them, without our interference. We create the structure or the vessel in this type of relationship. It is similar to the creation of a glass. We create a glass so that the water can be held and fulfill its purpose. But we are the glass, NOT the water. The water is given a place to fulfill itself through our embodiment as a Kabbalist. Our significant other, whether they are a parent, a spouse, a child or a friend, is then able to drink of their own unique essence. Over time, through the vessel of relationship, we are given a place to find our true self and share it with another.

A second beautiful Kabbalistic concept is the practice first taught by Issac Luria, which he called "binding to the spheres." In modern terms, this is about the embodiment of a quality within ourselves, the calling forward of a particular aspect which is needed by the other. We do not try to "give it" to the other. We just become it. And in the becoming of it, we provide a model for the other in a way that allows them to receive at whatever rate they can absorb. Most "healing" gone awry is the result of a willful imposition by the individual, believing that they know what is needed for the other. In the ultimate exemplification of the Hippocratic oath, Kabbalists simply embody a quality and allow it to seep out and percolate into the environment in non-intrusive ways.

For example, have you ever walked into a room and felt immediately there was "negativity" or "bad vibes?" A Kabbalist will merely look around and search for what quality is missing in this environment, and then cleave to it within themselves, embody it themselves, become it themselves. If the environment is chaotic and frantic, the Kabbalist embodies grounded, laser-like quietude, without "doing" anything to anyone, without processing any emotion, without psychologizing, without negotiating, but simply by becoming the thing that is necessary.

One of the many exquisite and beautiful aspects of Kabbalah is that every relationship becomes a vessel for healing. There is no loss of energy, no depletion, only nourishment and fulfillment for all involved. And through the embodiment of Divine qualities, we have an opportunity to be in spiritual practice in everyday life regardless of whether we are at work or at home, in spiritual community or at the bus station. We want to sanctify daily life and make every single thing we do sacred, since a Kabbalist and a practical mystic knows that only by bringing the Divine to our everyday lives will we ever truly find the happiness we seek.

Ultimately, the meticulous map of the unseen world provided by the Kabbalistic teachings has the potential to teach us about the deepest sources of physical, psychological, and spiritual healing, not just for those of Jewish ancestry but for all who seek relief from suffering. Yet the Jewish culture has seen the departure of many great and beautiful souls who have lost a connection to anything of relevance to their lives from their own tradition. The Kabbalah provides a return path home that brings new meaning, depth and spiritual light to a world filled with suffering. Within these teachings are the resources and options for every possible human struggle. And in this most amazing and difficult time in human history, we need all the help we can get to find the nourishment and support required to live a meaningful and fulfilling life.

Esoterica:
Kabbalah/Jewish Mysticism

REB LEIB HACOHEN: TEN REASONS

COMMENT:

The underlying map of the universe is known as the Tree of Life in Kabbalah. This map *(see diagram on page 13)* is a foundational teaching for the organization of the world, seen and unseen. The basic building blocks of the tree are the ten qualities or sephirot, as they are known in Hebrew. It is beyond the scope of this book to discuss in detail the tree of life, but by knowing this map, Kabbalah provides a resource for all imbalance to be understood. Through its study, we can even know what is needed to bring ourselves back into balance. Sometimes we are capable of doing it ourselves, sometimes we need help and sometimes it is not possible, for reasons known only to the Divine One. Below is an esoteric Kabbalistic text of why the soul loses connection with God, using the ten sephirot as its basis. The word Ego in this context is defined as the sum personality of the individual, while the Soul is seen as the spirit of the individual.

TEN REASONS

There is a window separating the Soul from the Kingdom of God, and there are ten reasons why it is shut:

1. The window remains shut because the Ego does not know it is there. This is the condition of Malkut, the 10th sefirah of the Tree of Life.

2. The window remains shut because the Ego, even knowing it is there, does not wish to open it. This is the condition of Yesod, the 9th sephirah of the Tree of Life.

3. The window remains shut because the Ego, knowing it is there and wishing to open it, does not know how to do so. This is the condition of Hod, the 8th sephirah of the Tree of Life.

4. The window remains shut because the Ego, knowing it is there, wishing to open it, and knowing how—is too large to pass through to the other side. This is the condition of Netzach, the 7th sephirah of the Tree of Life.

5. The window remains shut because the Ego, knowing it is there, wishing to open it, knowing how, and being small enough to pass through to the other side—is too weak to withstand the forces it will encounter there. This is the condition of Tipheret, the 6th sephirah of the Tree of Life.

6. The window remains shut because the Ego, knowing it is there, wishing to open it, knowing how, being small enough to pass through, having the strength to withstand the forces it will encounter on the other side—does not know where to turn when it gets there. This is the condition of Gevurah, the 5th sephirah of the Tree of Life.

7. The window remains shut because the Ego, knowing it is there, wishing to open it, knowing how, being small enough to pass through, having the strength to withstand the forces it will encounter on the other side and knowing where to turn when it gets there—has not notified the Elohim on the other side of its arrival. This is the condition of Chesed, the 4th sephirah of the Tree of Life.

8. The window remains shut because the Ego, knowing it is there, wishing to open it, knowing how, being small enough to pass through, having the strength to withstand the forces it will encounter on the other side, knowing where to turn when it gets there, and having notified the Elohim of its arrival—doubts that it is really there. This is the condition of Binah, the 3rd sephirah of the Tree of Life.

9. The window remains shut because the Ego, knowing it is there, wishing to open it, knowing how, being small enough to pass through, having the strength to withstand the forces it will encounter on the other side, knowing where to turn when it gets there, having notified the Elohim of its arrival, and having no doubts that it is there—hesitates to come alone and unaided before the Throne of Glory. This is the condition of Chockmah, the 2nd sephirah of the Tree of Life.

10. The window remains shut because the Ego, knowing it is there, wishing to open it, knowing how, being small enough to pass through, having the strength to withstand the forces it will encounter on the other side, knowing where to turn when it gets there and having notified the Elohim of its arrival, doesn't doubt that it is really there, and has come alone and unaided before the Throne of Glory—has

not yet been called by the Divine One. This is the condition of Keter, the 1st sephirah of the Tree of Life.

Note: Reb Leib HaCohen is the rebbe/founder of Donmeh West, an inclusive Kabbalistic teaching community. Please see the resource section in the back of this book for more information.

Christianity: A Course in Miracles and Theosophy

Maryann Williamson brought the popularity of A Course in Miracles to mainstream America. Yet the teachings, the curriculum so to speak, was written long before. Some believe that the course is literally the modern day "upgrade" of the biblical teachings of Jesus. While this remains debatable, there can be no debate on the profound nature of the work. It is designed to confront belief systems, open the heart, and change the way one lives in the world, one day at a time. Written as a teaching for each of the 365 days of the year, the path is woven with the reality that nothing is what it seems and that all is founded on Divine Intelligence.

For those who consider themselves to be Christian, yet have become disillusioned with religion, A Course in Miracles (*please see the resource section at the back of this book for more information on this work*) provides mystical understanding of the teachings of Jesus which can be life-changing without the trappings of religious ritual.

Long before the Course in Miracles, a young Christian woman named Alice Bailey began to teach about the mysteries of the unseen world. Her teacher called himself The Tibetan, and therefore her work is flavored with the taste of Eastern Spirituality. Alice Bailey wrote volumes and her work is a great resource to those who wish to understand the esoteric world.

Esoterica:
Theosophy/Christian Mysticism

ALICE BAILEY: KARMIC LIABILITIES

COMMENT:

Each individual has a tendency to fall into certain patterns relative to their difficulties in life. These primal patterns of distortion arise in seekers of consciousness as they awaken. By identifying the pattern, then consciously watching for it, and changing it when it happens, we begin to restructure ourselves at a basic level through awareness and intention.

Foundational causes of our suffering can be found in these seven themes and our challenge is to see ourselves within them.

FROM ESOTERIC HEALING BY ALICE BAILEY
LAW IX

Perfection calls imperfection to the surface. The method used by the Perfect One and that employed by Good is harmlessness. This is not negativity, but perfect poise, a completed point of view and divine understanding.

THE SEVEN RAY CAUSES OF INHARMONY AND DISEASE

1. The Initiate set Himself to follow by Himself alone his chosen path. He brooked no interference. He hardened His courses. From plane to plane, this hardening proceeded; it grew and stiffened. His will was set, and crystal-like, brilliant, brittle and hard. The power to crystallize was His. He brought not will-to-live but will-to-die. Death was his gift to life. Infusion and diffusion pleased Him not. He loved and sought abstraction.

2. The Initiate poured His life throughout all parts and every aspect of manifestation. From the center to the periphery and from the periphery to the center He rushed, carrying abundance of life, energizing all forms of Himself, producing excess of movement, endless extension, abundant growth and undue haste. He knew not what He wanted, because He wanted all, desired all, attracted all and gave to all too much.

3. The Initiate gathered here and there. He chose and He rejected. This power He refused and this power He accepted. He had no purpose linked to the six purposes of His six Brothers. He acquired a form and liked it not; threw it away and chose another. He had no settled point or plan but lived in glamour and liked it well. He smothered both the good and the bad, though using both. Excess in one direction could be seen and starvation in another. Both these extremes governed His choice of living substance, He threw together those that suited not each other, then saw the end was sorrow and deceit. Patterns He made, but purpose suited not. He gave up in despair.

4. The Initiate fought and entered into combat. All that He met appeared to him a subject for display of power. Within the fourth He found a field of battle and settled down to fight. He saw the right and knew the wrong and vibrated between the two, fighting first the one and then the other, but missing all the time that midway point where battle is not known. There harmony, ease and rest and peaceful silence will be found. He weakened all the forms which used His strength and power. Yet all the time he sought for beauty; searched for loveliness; and yearned for peace. Despair overtook Him in His courses, and with despair the will-to-live could not survive. Yet all the time the loveliness was there.

5. The Initiate arose in His wrath and separated Himself. He swept aside the great dualities and saw primarily the field of multiplicity. He produced cleavage on every hand. He wrought with potent thought for separative action. He established barriers with joy. He brooked no understanding; He knew no unity, for He was cold, austere, ascetic and forever cruel. He stood between the tender, loving center of all lives and the outer court of writhing, living men. Yet He stood not at the midway point,

and naught He did sufficed to heal the breach. He widened all cleavages, erected barriers, and sought to make still wider gaps.

6. The Initiate loved Himself in others and in all forms. On every hand, He saw objects of His devotion and ever they proved to be Himself. Into these others He ever poured Himself, asking response and never getting it. Surely and with certainty the outlines of the forms so loved were lost, grew dim and disappeared. The objects of His love slowly faded out. Only a world of shadows, of mist and fog remained. And as He looked upon Himself, He said: Lord of Glamour, that am I, and the Angel of Bewilderment. Naught is clear to me. I love yet all seems wrong! I know that love is right and the spirit of the universe. What then is wrong?

7. The Initiate gathered to Himself His forces and affirmed His intention to create. He created that which is outer and can be seen. He saw His creations and liked them not and so withdrew His attention; then the creations He made died and disappeared. He had no lasting success and saw naught but failure as He traveled on the outer path of life. He comprehended naught the need of forms. To some He gave an over-plus of life, to some too little; and so both kinds died and failed to show the beauty of the Lord Who gave them life but failed to give them understanding. He knew naught then that love sustains.

Note: Alice Bailey was a theosophical mystic who lived in the early 1900's. Her prolific work is now distributed by Lucis Press. Please see the resource section in the back of this book for more information.

On Sufism

If you are reading this book, you probably consider yourself to be a "spiritual-type" in some way. Perhaps you are more discrete about it, preferring to keep your beliefs to yourself. Or maybe you are right out there in the spotlight with your ideas. Either way, it is likely that you believe there is something greater than what meets the eye in this life here on earth.

Over the course of my own life, I have come to deeply believe in the validity of the unseen world. I have also come to believe that every soul has a particular spiritual path that it resonates with most deeply, just as we have colors we prefer and music we like. I want to speak about one path in particular, since if you have tasted the smorgasbord of spiritual paths but have not found one that is just right for you, this might just be the one. And even if it is not, this is a chance to learn more about a path that has remained relatively obscure in America despite the recent revival of many traditional teachings. This path is called the Sufi path, and has a great deal of both mystery and confusion around it.

Though I am a Jewish soul, I spent several years living with the Sufis in both Jerusalem, Israel and the United States. At one point I was designated as a muqaddam, or representative teacher and spiritual leader for a community of Sufis. Though ultimately I left due to philosophical disagreements and because I am a Jew, not a Muslim, the knowledge I gained there was invaluable. Many in our world might find their spiritual home in the Sufi tradition and to this end I share with you a few tidbits about the path. If you want to learn more, please see the resource section in the back of this book.

Most people familiar with Sufism are likely to think of Sufi dancing. Yet this is just a minor expression of one stream of Sufism, an ancient mystical path embodying great depth and wisdom. Sufism is rooted in the Persian/Arabic culture of the 12th century, when many of the great mystics and scholars began to teach throughout the world. The famous poet Rumi is an example of one such mystic, but there are many others with equal beauty and richness. And although Sufism is usually based in the tradition of Islam, it is based in a type of Islam that very few in the western world truly understand. The Islam of the Sufis is the tradition of the embodiment of Divine Love.

It is important for all seekers of truth to understand that the true teachings of Islam have been distorted and twisted by human beings over the centuries, resulting in a depiction of that religion as conflictive and often chauvinistic. The original teachings of the prophet Muhammad have been utilized to justify the most inhumane acts. Sadly, all Muslims pay the price for the actions of a few. A minor percentage of Islamic extremist groups promote the violence we have seen in recent years. Yet the entire Muslim world has been stigmatized. Sadly also, the response by Muslim clerics has been to become more orthodox rather than more tolerant, in an understandable attempt to protect their communities. Having lived among the Muslim people for years of my life, I found them to be deeply loving and compassionate people who long for connection and understanding. The Islamic Sufis I know are people wishing to change the way the western world sees Islam and they often wish to bring the voice of compassion and understanding to the table. These Sufis utilize the original teachings of the Prophet to support deep equality among people and peace-loving practices of coexistence and tolerance. During my time in the Middle East, they were the ones who were willing to risk life and limb to sit among Christians and Jews, each praying in the manner of their own faith, yet gathering in the same place. It is their impeccable devotion to their faith and to their belief in the possibility of a different world that allows them to do these things. The Sufis base their lives on love, service and the alleviation of the suffering of humanity.

Part of the Sufi teaching is to make oneself invisible in the environment and to continuously ask the question, "What is needed here to bring balance and peace to the situation, and to infuse it with love?" Over the centuries the Sufis have been known for integrating the local culture of the area to the traditional practices, to avoid separation or superiority. This is as true now as it was in the 12th century in the days of Ibn Arabi, often believed to be the greatest Sufi to have ever lived. Sufism teaches to live in the world that we inhabit rather than retreat to a mountaintop in seclusion.

Most Sufis pray frequently. They chant and drum, and worship in many forms, but from a place of choice rather than a place of obligation or empty dogma. In fact, in the Sufi way that I studied, it was forbidden to take on a spiritual practice until the yearning of the heart was strong enough. This may take years. And once taken on—it is taken on as a disciple—the true source of the word discipline. Sufis set a minimal regular practice for themselves and try to maintain it to the best of their ability, even when they are not feeling up to it in the moment at hand. They are taught to not respond to impulse (Sufis call this the nafs) but to the Voice of the Divine within. One prayer a day done with conviction is better than three prayers a day done with resentment and obligation, since they know in the long run all three will be abandoned if there is no depth or meaning. In this way, a realistic minimal practice is maintained which is honored despite varying emotional and mental states.

Sufis are often known for their ecstatic reveries and the bliss of God that is called for in their gatherings. The most famous of these practices is called zikr, a group chant with drums and body movement that intentionally creates a trance-like state. For some this practice can be uncomfortable, since it can be extremely ungrounding. But for most, it is the source of their delight and joy.

If you have longed for a spiritual path that embraces art and poetry and dance and surrender into the Divine, Sufism is the place to find all of that and more. The Sufi soul finds nourishment in community and creative expression, as well as verbal and ecstatic praise to the Divine. I invite you to seek out the Sufis if your heart is longing for expression in this way. Choose wisely, and thoughtfully, always listening to the voice of truth inside. But if you find you long for a means of Divine worship that includes the body, mind and soul, the Sufi way is one beautiful possibility.

Into the arms of the Master, His beloved surrenders everything.

— *anonymous Sufi quote*

Esoterica:
Sufism/Islamic Mysticism

ABDUL KARIM AL-JILI: UNIVERSAL MAN

COMMENT:

This work is considered to be a systematic exposition of the teachings of the great Sufi Ibn Arabi. Below you will find a text translated by Titus Burckhardt which speaks about the nature of Divine revelation and the qualities required by an individual in order to have a direct experience of the Divine.

UNIVERSAL MAN

Amongst those who realize the Divine Word, some understand hidden things; so they have knowledge of events before they happen, be it that they know in reply to their questions, and it is that which happens most often, or be it that God warns them on His own initiative.

Others of those who realize this Divine Quality ask for miracles, and God gratifies them, so that they have proof of Him when they return to their corporal conscience while still keeping their attitude towards God. May these examples suffice for that which is the participation of the Divine Word.

We return then to the unveiling of the Divine Qualities in general. Amongst those who contemplate them, there are some to whom God reveals Himself by the Volitive Quality, so that the creations are in proportion to the will of the servant. The fact is that on receiving the Divine revelation in the Quality of the Word, the servant wants, by the Unity of this Quality, that which he realizes of the creation, and it is thus that things exist by his will. Many of those who attain this state of contemplation draw back, so that they end by denying that which they have perceived of God. The servant who, ravished in the world of Divine Mystery, has contemplated things, in an Essential vision, as existing by his own will, and who then returns to his exterior conscience, is tempted to look again for this same relationship between himself and things (on the individual plane). Then, as he does not find it again, he rejects his Essential contemplation and goes backwards. Immediately the glass which contains the lamp of his heart is broken, and he comes to deny God after having contemplated Him, to lose Him after having found Him.

Note: Abdul Karim Al-Jili lived in the middle ages and was considered to be one of the greatest commentators on the work of Ibn Arabi. Please see the resource section in the back of this book for more information.

SECTION V: SPIRITUAL TEACHERS

_____

Each progressive spirit is opposed by a thousand mediocre minds appointed to guard the past.

— Maurice Maeterlinck

Introduction

The reflections you will read in this section are a result of deep and personal experiences with teachers of several traditions…both good teachers and teachers who have abused their power. Having had the experience of both, I have the good fortune of being able to contrast the qualities of an "honorable" teacher or mentor, with one who is abusing their authority, perhaps to the point of being dangerous.

Research in the area of abuse of power repeatedly shows that certain personality patterns and qualities tend to be common among the two different groups. Since we are ultimately responsible for selecting our teachers, my intention is to provide as much information so the reader might choose wisely and have the courage to identify a power abuser, or at least be able to recognize positive and negative transference with a teacher. The goal is not to avoid having a teacher or mentor, but instead to find one who acts with honor and integrity, and who encourages spiritual autonomy, personal responsibility and right action in the world.

I believe very strongly that one should have places of spiritual accountability and places where personality patterns can be identified by an objective other. Individuals who claim they no longer need such things, that they are "enlightened" or that they have "direct guidance" from the Divine are often the most dangerous, since there is no mechanism for accountability or for the identification of self-deception. A wise soul will be rooted in accountability while maintaining a spiritual autonomy which is true to the nature of their soul.

Discernment: Choosing An Honorable Teacher

The archetype of the abusive spiritual teacher appears in many forms. From the spiritual "master" who sleeps with his students; to the Christian charismatic who leads his people to stockpile weapons; to the evangelist who ultimately drinks poisonous Kool Aid with his community, we are in a time when an honorable teacher and an untrustworthy one are difficult to tell apart. And since all are human, how can one ever know? And is it even of value to have a teacher in these times anyhow?

These are legitimate questions that require deep and thorough inquiry. Perhaps we can start by looking at the dynamics of how good-hearted, decent, intelligent people can be led astray. The issue here is not about intelligence, but about the deep and profound yearning to know God. The spiritual thirst in our time and in our country is palpable. Unfortunately, deceivers can become powerful with a minimal understanding of human psychology. In a culture such as ours which considers religious leaders as authority figures, and values the external world more than the inner life, it takes only one who speaks with authority and conviction to create a fertile environment in which to seduce the hungry soul who seeks God. Therefore, it behooves the seeker to search for a teacher using an informed mind and with open eyes.

Recently, wonderful research has been done on the concept of the cult of the personality. Since this word "cult" is riddled with drama and extremes, we must be careful about definitions. But for the sake of this discussion, I would suggest that the term "cult of the personality" is a phrase that best suits the dynamic of a community where there is one central charismatic leader who represents him or her self as the ultimate authority or who is the originator of an ideology or spiritual path and presents themselves as the final "knower." In fact, this may be one distinguishing factor that helps to discern the difference between a true spiritual teacher and one who leads from ego—this factor being that a true teacher will never represent themselves as the final authority for God. They will always return personal power and autonomy to the individual and will never demand complete compliance without question.

A cult of the personality, on the other hand, forbids either explicitly or covertly, the questioning of the leader or disagreement with any of the teachings. Any dissent is seen as an affront to the leader, impolite or disrespectful, rather than as a legitimate inquiry for discerning truth.

Other warning signs include a teacher who represents himself as a human voice for the Divine; an exclusionary philosophy towards other traditions; an insistence that the teacher's path is the highest, best or most Divine, while others are seen as astray in some form; a subtle culture of detaching from those who are not part of the philosophy and escaping from the world toward like-minded companions only; an insistence on financial support of the leader, frequently to the exclusion of other charitable causes; an unwillingness of the leadership to provide financial disclosure, especially in nonprofit organizations; and a general sense of superiority by those who involve themselves in this particular tradition.

All of these qualities should be warning bells for the seeker of Truth. They are examples of spiritual glamour at best, and spiritual betrayal and breech of trust at worst. The heart of the seeker always knows Truth. When one is encouraged to not listen to the heart, but to listen to the authority, the subtle removing of personal power and autonomy begins. This can only be a set up for more difficulties.

Most sadly, as a result of an encounter with an unethical teacher, many people turn away from a spiritual path of any form. Many lose trust in even a basic human relationship, and become more confused and disillusioned, rather than more conscious.

The alternative is to prepare the eye, by educating the heart and by beginning to trust the inner Truth that always knows what is good and right. A true teacher will always return their student to this reality, and teach them how to listen to their own inner wisdom. They will not provide instant gratification, sensory "initiation" experience based in glamour, or make decisions for their students about their daily life or business activities. They will lead the person back to themselves rather than take the power from their soul. They will remain an open system, admit when they are wrong, apologize when necessary and continuously seek for the best in themselves as well as their students. A good teacher is self-responsible and will own their limitations, errors and defects.

In addition, a good teacher will have a teacher of their own, in physical form, to coach and mentor them. Ideally, they will be in a personal process with someone outside of the system where they can work on their own issues and shadow aspects. A teacher who avoids shadow work, or who works with someone inside the system, can easily delude themselves into believing that they are sincerely doing their work, when in fact they are not. Or worse, they can come to believe that they are beyond the laws of society or the world in general.

A truly enlightened individual lives in the outer world as well as in the unseen worlds with balance and harmony, without ignoring the personality or the body and its inevitable imperfections. They will never place themselves beyond the law. And they will never need to speak about their spiritual status to anyone. Therefore, to a trained eye, an honorable teacher will stand out quite clearly from the rest.

It is not possible for the doors of the invisible world to be opened while the heart craves for them. We will only truly see when we come to terms as a culture with our cravings for power and thrills and when we let go of our misconceptions about freedom.

— Ibn Arabi

Tony Soprano and Spiritual Teachers

The dynamics of spiritual power, and of power in general, are both mysterious and obvious at the same time. What is it that drives people to travel thousands of miles, or give over their life savings to a spiritual teacher? Innumerable spiritual seekers every year, people who are considered relatively normal, take such drastic actions. Though there are many answers to this question, a primal theme prevails. The experts call it The Balm of Love.

Each and every one of us has a deep-seated need to be loved and accepted, to be seen for who we are and to be known at our essence. When a spiritual teacher comes along who can provide such a response, the magnetic pull can be overwhelming. This is where Tony Soprano comes in. While I originally was not a fan of the popular television show "The Sopranos," the first night I decided to take a look at what the world was raving about, some striking revelations began to arise like an epiphany. In front of my eyes, the dynamics of disowned power were being played out right there on HBO. In return for a hefty money contribution, every member of The Family was provided with love, safety, respect and belonging. And as long as everyone played by the rules, the system worked impeccably. But what happens when the barter requires doing something that is against the ethic of the individual? Within the Family system, if the individual insists on following his own truth, he is usually killed off. Most often, the individual acquiesces, and a small part of his soul is given up in exchange for safety and the comfort of the group. This primal need almost always wins over, even though the essence of the soul is chipped away little by little. As you can see, these concepts do not just apply to spiritual teachers, but to any system where the leader has not addressed his or her own unconscious power needs.

And so it goes with distorted spiritual leadership—an energetic and spiritual bribe is established. In exchange for complete surrender to the decisions and the norms of the leader, the individual receives social safety, the comfort of a group and the sense of specialness that feeds the wound of inadequacy which is the plague of our society. All that is necessary is loyal compliance, ignoring of the truth of the heart which may be in contradiction, and the leaving of family and friends who are not involved with the teacher.

With these guidelines, isn't Tony Soprano a prime candidate to become the next spiritual leader of our spiritually hungry society?

Some of us have unwittingly arrived at the doorstep of a teacher who abuses power. When the inevitable day arrives that the individual can no longer neglect what their heart knows, can no longer betray themselves and can no longer follow something that is against their ethic; when that individual realizes that it is not their lower self speaking, but their inner instincts; when one sees this reality though everyone around them convinces them otherwise, what are they to do? How does one leave "the Family" without getting killed?

There is only one answer. Walk away. Walk with grace and dignity. Do not insult the leader. Do not listen to a single word that is said by the Family. Their investment is in keeping you, since if you agree with them, they cannot be wrong. Thousands of people in this world have died because they needed to feel "right," even if they were not. If you leave, it might make them doubt their own decisions as well. So do not try to explain, convince, defend or change the Family. Just walk away and know that Truth is eternal and a lie is temporary, even if it seems eternal. It is not. In the greater cycle of life, it cannot survive, though it may grow in the short run.

Believe what your heart is telling you even if no one else can confirm it for you. Honor the freedom you have to believe the truth of the heart and know that there is no greater spiritual path than courageously listening to the truth of your heart and acting on it in every moment. If you can find it, walk towards a place that acknowledges struggle and welcomes disagreement and differences. Believe that over time you will find a place where people love God and can disagree, where "purification" is not a theme that indicates cutting things out. Humanity cannot be amputated, or discharged, only embraced by an aware central self that sees each part as Divine or attempting to be Divine even when it is causing problems in the moment. By developing the capacity to hold the tension of the opposites, a Third Thing is allowed to emerge, a place where one person's truth does not negate the truth of another. Where one person's practice is not better, higher, purer or more in alignment than another. Where every being, every child, every family member, is held precious, regardless of their philosophy, their religion, their sexual preference or their so-called "spiritual station."

Find a place—or create one—where preciousness is the theme, truth is the theme, freedom is the theme. Allow for the fact that sometimes it is not pretty, sometimes it is messy and disagreement abounds. Sometimes there is struggle and discomfort. But do not accept substitutes. True spiritual contact, true leadership, true community does not place the value of one person over another. True spiritual leadership will lead you back to yourself as the highest authority, not back to the leader. It will provide you with tools to be more of who you really are, not less. It will make you feel confident in the world whether you are in community or alone, in Japan or France or Hawaii. And there is never, ever money involved in exchange for elevating your spiritual state, which is in reality, only God's territory. And truly, your spiritual state is no one's business other than your own.

SECTION VI: THE FEMALE MYSTIC

Introduction

I have saved this section for the end. The way of the female mystic is, I believe, an essential aspect of the future. Only through the rightful return of the female psyche to the essence of spirituality, not just as student, but as teacher, as co-creator, as an awakened, creative force for change, will our world continue to thrive and grow.

The following three pieces are a reflection of that direction. The first piece is believed by some to have been written by Mary Magdalene. It is part of the Gospel of Mary in the Nag Hammadi Library. These scrolls were discovered in a cave in the 1940's and are only now beginning to be translated and published in English. They reveal much about the hidden aspects of the female mystic and they are some of the only ancient texts known to be written by a woman. Their pearls are for all of us. For the sake of brevity I have presented only certain sections, but the entire text can be found in the Nag Hammadi Library Resources. The second is my own call for the return of the Divine Feminine into the consciousness of our world. The third piece is a spontaneous prayer in the spirit of the female mystic that nourishes the modern soul in a new and profound way. May you drink from this well of immersion in the Feminine Face of the Divine and know that this too, is God.

Thunder Perfect Mind

Thunder Perfect Mind *is a marvelous, strange poem. It speaks in the voice of a feminine divine power, but one that unites all opposites. One that is not only speaking in women, but also in all people. One that speaks not only in citizens, but aliens, it says, in the poor and in the rich. It's a poem which sees the radiance of the divine in all aspects of human life, from the sordidness of the slums of Cairo or Alexandria, as they would have been, to the people of great wealth, from men to women to slaves. In that poem, the divine appears in every, and the most unexpected of forms....*

— Elaine Pagels
FRONTLINE

Thunder Perfect Mind

Translated by George W. MacRae

I was sent forth from the power,
And I have come to those who reflect upon me,
And I have been found among those who seek after me.
Look upon me, you who reflect upon me,
And you hearers, hear me.
You who are waiting for me, take me to yourselves.
And do not banish me from your sight.
And do not make your voice hate me, nor your hearing.
Do not be ignorant of me anywhere or any time. Be on your guard!
Do not be ignorant of me.
For I am the first and the last.
I am the honored one and the scorned one.
I am the whore and the holy one.
I am the wife and the virgin.
I am the mother and the daughter.
I am the members of my mother.
I am the barren one
And many are her sons.
I am she whose wedding is great,
And I have not taken a husband.
I am the midwife and she who does not bear.
I am the solace of my labor pains.
I am the bride and the bridegroom,

And it is my husband who begot me.
I am the mother of my father
And the sister of my husband
And he is my offspring.
I am the slave of him who prepared me.
I am the ruler of my offspring.
But he is the one who begot me before the time on a birthday.
And he is my offspring in (due) time,
And my power is from him.
I am the staff of his power in his youth,
And he is the rod of my old age.
And whatever he wills happens to me.
I am the silence that is incomprehensible
And the idea whose remembrance is frequent.
I am the voice whose sound is manifold
And the word whose appearance is multiple.
I am the utterance of my name.
......
Do not hate my obedience
And do not love my self-control.
In my weakness, do not forsake me,
And do not be afraid of my power.
For why do you despise my fear
And curse my pride?
But I am she who exists in all fears
And strength in trembling.
......
I am she who is weak,
And I am well in a pleasant place.
I am senseless and I am wise.
......
I am the one that you have despised,
And you reflect upon me.
I am the one whom you have hidden from,
And you appear to me.
But whenever you hide yourselves,
I myself will appear.
For whenever you appear,
I myself will hide from you.

......

And take me to yourselves from places that are ugly and in ruin,
And rob from those which are good even though in ugliness.
Out of shame, take me to yourselves shamelessly;
And out of shamelessness and shame,
Upbraid my members in yourselves.
And come forward to me, you who know me
And you who know my members,
And establish the great ones among the small first creatures.
Come forward to childhood,
And do not despise it because it is small and it is little.
And do not turn away greatnesses in some parts from the smallnesses,
For the smallnesses are known from the greatnesses.
Look then at his words
And all the writings which have been completed.
Give heed then, you hearers
And you also, the angels and those who have been sent,
And you spirits who have arisen from the dead.
For I am the one who alone exists,
And I have no one who will judge me.
For many are the pleasant forms which exist in numerous sins,
And incontinencies, and disgraceful passions, and fleeting pleasures,
Which (men) embrace until they become sober
And go up to their resting place.
And they will find me there,
And they will live,
And they will not die again.

— James M. Robinson, ed.
The Nag Hammadi Library, revised edition.
HarperCollins, San Francisco, 1990

Making a Place in the World for the Female Mystic

My mom was the first feminist in my life. She always encouraged me to make my own way in the world and to stand courageously for my beliefs. This advice has faired me well. But as I became an adult learner and seeker, I made some interesting discoveries. The most potent was that despite the progress we have made as a culture, there was a marked gap in female leadership in the world of religious and spiritual teachers. Yes, there was an occasional female guru or Buddhist nun, an occasional courageous feminist rabbi or shaykha, but in general the world of spiritual and religious knowledge was filled with male teachers and female students. This remains the case even to this day.

Ironically, I would not call myself a feminist. I find that the image I carry of a feminist is not a positive one in any way—an angry, man-hating woman carrying a grudge like a weapon. While I am certain that this image is quite outdated, and one that many current-day feminists do not embody, that old approach of attacking the other in order to feel powerful seems woven into many of our psyches. It is not the way we will find a place for the Divine Feminine. As a woman, I love the men of the world. They are as much a victim of the societal patriarchy as the women. Most of them are just doing what they have been taught. Rather, I would prefer to nourish and encourage women to love men, to be powerful and to stand in their essence with strength and softness; being gentle and mighty at the same time; not budging on the important issues; not bashing those who disagree; allowing a place at the table for everyone to be who they are, what they are, right now, right here; not separating themselves from men in order to be insulated from the inevitable protest; not giving up their soul for the sake of someone else's belief about what is right. And ultimately, not surrendering their essence for the sake of peace at the expense of truth.

The inevitable protest to embodying these qualities can usually be traced back to a lie about power, or women, or what God wants, or feeling safe in the world. The inevitable protest must be withstood long enough for the truth to emerge. It is the hardest and yet most necessary challenge of the men and women who are awake in the world. All the great ones did it. Rosa Parks did it for the African American community. Susan B. Anthony did it in the political community. Now we must do it in the spiritual community.

For the conscious men in the world, the challenge is great—to allow and call forward the women of the world to be a partner, a co-creator, a sharer of power. And to rejoice in that partnership, knowing that the true power of the Divine Feminine is not a power that will annihilate, it is one that will nourish, fortify and uplift everything and everyone in its sphere.

When I look around for this model, it remains elusive. The female mystic is a rare and uncommon species. Perhaps it is just that she has been hidden. The male rabbis I know often speak of the hidden female behind the prophets. But again I ask, what good does that do? The lack of written history or documentation about female leadership reflects the prevailing psyche, the unconscious wish to let the female mystic be invisible, hidden, mysteriously unknown.

It is time for the Divine Feminine to come out of the closet. We must not be ashamed and we must not be angry or aggressive. Or rather I would say, we must do our consciousness work with the parts that are ashamed and the parts that are angry and aggressive, carrying them as a friend but not letting them dictate our actions. We must become women who just know we are powerful, with no need to prove it. We must be able to weave into the community and at the same time speak with gentleness and might when the time is right. We must forgive the men of the world for having been taught a lie. And we must teach them a new story, a new truth—that women can be powerful and still love their men. That they can be strong, sexy, brave and autonomous—and still remain in relationship. That they have no need to reign over anything, but they have the capacity to know, to teach and to lead in a very different way.

The Kabbalah teaches that there is an underlying blueprint of the world called the Tree of Life (*see diagram on page 13*). On this tree, there are ten foundational emanations that lie beneath the fabric of the world. The last of these emanations is called Malkut, or the kingdom. Malkut is considered to be a feminine aspect of God. Perhaps it should have been called the Queendom. Nevertheless, this aspect is the final piece that finishes the creation of the world. It is feminine. It represents the physical, the tangible, the earth, the womb, the raw material of the world, the blood, the dirt, the components of the world that have often been given a less-than-holy definition. Yet it is the required element for the completion of anything. It is the holy last step in the process of manifestation. Without Malkut, nothing is manifested, nothing is finished, and nothing has an existence. Without Malkut, the world would not exist. Without the Mother, the child would not exist.

It is time for the female mystic to take her place, for the woman Kabbalist, the Zen Buddhist, the Christian Gnostic and the Sufi mystic to stand up, come out of the darkness and let her voice, gentle and mighty, be heard. Not at the expense of all the beautiful men in the world. Not in a rebellious or angry manner. But with grace and poise and dignity, with juiciness and delight, eternally cherishing the men of the world, taking nothing from them, robbing them of nothing. But standing fully next to them and not behind them or under them. Being fully present, knowing and holding this place of Divine Power. When the thunder of opposition rises up, to remain clear, calm, and steadfast. And through it all, to be gentle and mighty.

Because without the female mystic, the path of God is unfinished.

Wild Prayer

I'm happy to announce that this is a perfect moment.

It's a perfect moment for many reasons, but especially
because I have been inspired to say a gigantic prayer
for all of you. I've been roused to unleash a divinely
greedy, apocalyptically healing prayer for each and
every one of you—even those of you who don't
believe in the power of prayer.

And so I am starting to pray right now to the God of Gods...
the God beyond all Gods...the Girlfriend of God...
the Teacher of God...the Goddess who invented God.

Dear Goddess, You who never kill but only change:

I pray that my exuberant, suave and accidental words
will move you to shower ferocious blessings down on
everyone who reads this benediction.

I pray that you will give them what they don't even
know they want—not just the boons they think they
need but everything they've always been afraid to even
imagine or ask for.

Dear Goddess, You wealthy anarchist burning heaven to the ground:

Many of the divine chameleons out there don't even
know that their souls will live forever. So please use
your blinding magic to help them see that they are all
wildly creative geniuses too big for their own personalities.

Guide them to realize that they are all completely
different from what they think they are and more
exciting than they can possibly imagine.

Make it illegal, immoral, irrelevant, unpatriotic and
totally tasteless for them to be in love with anyone
or anything that's no good for them.

O Goddess, You who give us so much love and pain mixed
together that our morality is always on the verge of collapsing:

I beg you to cast a huge-assed love spell that will
nullify all the dumb ideas, bad decisions and nasty
conditioning that have ever cursed the wise and sexy
virtuosos out there.

Remove, banish, annihilate and laugh into oblivion any
jinx that has clung to them, no matter how long
they've suffered from it, and even if they've become
accustomed or addicted to its ugly companionship.

And please conjure an aura of protection around them
so that they will receive an early warning if they are
ever about to act in such a way as to bring another
hex or plague or voodoo into their lives in the future.

Dear Goddess, sweet Goddess, You sly universal beautiful woman:

Arouse the Wild Woman within them—even if they're men.

And please give them bigger, better, more original
sins and wilder, more interesting problems.

Dear Goddess, I pray that you will inspire all the compassionate
rascals communing with this prayer to love their
enemies just in case their friends turn out to be jerks.

Provoke them to throw away or give away all the things
they own that encourage them to believe that they are
better than anyone else.

Most of all, Goddess, brainwash them with your freedom
so that they never love their own pain more than anyone else's pain.

Dear Goddess, You psychedelic mushroom cloud
at the center of all our brains:

The curiously divine human beings reading this prayer
deserve everything they are yearning for and much, much more.

So please bless them with lucid dreams while they are
wide awake and vacuum cleaners for their
magic carpets and a knack for avoiding other people's
hells and please bless them with a secret admirer who is
not a psychotic stalker.

Dear Goddess, You fiercely tender, hauntingly
reassuring, orgiastically sacred feeling that is even
now running through all of our soft, warm animal bodies:

I pray that you provide everyone out there with a
license to bend and even break all unholy rules, laws and
traditions that keep them apart from the things they love.

Show them how to purge the wishy-washy wishes that
distract them from their daring, dramatic, divine desires.

And teach them that they can have any good thing they want
if they'll only ask for it in an unselfish way.

And now dear God of Gods, God beyond all Gods, Girlfriend of God, Teacher of God, Goddess who invented God, I bring this prayer to a close, trusting that in these mysterious moments you have begun to change everyone out there in the exact way they've needed to change in order to express their soul's code.

Amen. Awomen. And glory hallelujah.

— Meghan Marwell
Santa Fe, NM
June, 2001
A spontaneous prayer on the occasion of a personal retreat

Resources and Websites

May you walk with equanimity in a world of chaos,
May your suffering be held with dignity,
May you find the abundant joy that results from Truth,
And may you always know that you are loved.

— Jodi Prinzivalli
New York City, NY
August 2004

Resources and Websites

CONTACT THE AUTHOR

Dr. Jodi Prinzivalli
Center for Healing and Energetic Psychology
70 Hilltop Road
Ramsey, NJ 07446
Websites: **www.energeticpsychology.com**
             www.interfaith-encounter.org
E-mail: jodiprinz@optonline.net
Phone: 201.851.4909

VOICE DIALOGUE/
WORK WITH THE UNCONSCIOUS MIND

Website: www.voicedialogue.org
Delos Incorporated, Voice Dialogue Training
and the work of Drs. Sidra and Hal Stone

Website: www.cil.org
Center For Intentional Living and the work of Alexis Johnson

KABBALAH/ KABBALISTIC HEALING

Website: www.kabbalah.org
A Society of Souls, Integrated Kabbalistic Healing,
and the work of Jason Shulman

Website: www.tirzahfirestone.com
The work of Rabbi Tirzah Firestone

Website: www.aleph.org
The work of Aleph, the Jewish Renewal Movement

OTHER SPIRITUAL RESOURCES

Website: www.lucispress.org
Lucis Press and the work of Alice Bailey

Website: www.acim.org
A Course in Miracles

Website: www.kenwilbur.com
The consciousness work of Ken Wilbur

Website: www.ibnarabi.org
The organization founded to study the work of Sufi mystic Ibn Arabi

Website: www.kebzeh.org
The work of the Kebzeh Sufi community and Murat Yagan

WHOLISTIC MEDICAL RESOURCES

Website: www.drslifeline.com
Lifeline Healing: A Chicago-based wholistic medical center utilizing the best
of energetic medicine

Website: www.life-enhancement.com
A high quality supplement and anti-aging medicine resource

Website: www.antiaging-systems.com
The International Association of Anti-Aging Medicine

ADDICTIONS/ EXIT COUNSELING

Website: www.milestonesretreat.com
Inpatient eating disorders treatment program

Website: www.aa.org
Alcoholics Anonymous

Website: www.freedomofmind.com
The work of Steven Hasan and Exit Counseling Resources

Website: www.wellspringretreat.org
Exit counseling inpatient retreat center

INTERFAITH RESOURCES

Website: www.interfaith-encounter.org
The Interfaith Encounter Association is dedicated to promoting coexistence
among the religions through interfaith dialogue and cross-cultural study.

Website: www.samedifference.org
The project of Same Difference, an interfaith performance, documentary film
and project based on several hundred anonymous and spontaneous interviews
of Jews, Muslims and Christians after 9/11.

Website: www.metasulha.org
The sulha is a traditional gathering where those of differing cultures and views come together to share music, food and thoughts of the heart. The Sulha movement carries the vision of conducting regular sulhas to facilitate coexistence among Muslims, Jews and Christians in the Holy Land.

Website: www.brucefeiler.org
As the author of the best-selling novel Abraham, Bruce Feiler offers a structured format for conducting interfaith gatherings on a local level.

Website: www.ume.org
The University of the Middle East is an institution of higher learning with campuses in Morocco, the United States and Spain. Its vision is to promote academic excellence, tolerance, dialogue and regional cooperation among religious cultures through mutual study and the educational experience.

Website: www.donmeh-west.org
The Donmeh West, founded and lead by Reb Yakov Leib HaCohen, weaves the many mystical traditions in a unique way through spiritual education and the practice of syncretic, neo-Sabbatian Kabbalah.

OTHER ASSORTED RESOURCES

Website: www.joelmeyerowitz.com
The work of Joel Meyerowitz, official photographer for Ground Zero.

SUGGESTED READING

Abraham. Bruce Feiler. (William Morrow 2002)

A Course In Miracles. Foundation for Inner Peace. (FIP Publishing 1975)

The Art of War. Sun Tzu. Edited by James Clavell. (Delacorte Press 1983).

Beyond Belief. Elaine Pagels. (Random House 2003)

Boundary and Space: An Introduction to the Work of Donald Winnicott. Edited by Madeleine Davis & David Wallbridge. (Brunner Mazel 1987)

The Collected Works of Ken Wilbur. Ken Wilbur. (Shamballa 1999)

The Dark Side of the Light Chasers. Debbie Ford. (Riverhead Books 1998)

Embracing Ourselves. Drs. Sidra and Hal Stone. (New World Publishing 1988)

Embracing Each Other. Drs. Sidra and Hal Stone. (Delos Publishing 1989)

Entrance to the Garden of Eden. Yossi Klein Halevi. (Perennial Publishing 2002)

The Elegant Universe. Brian Green. (Vintage Books 1999)

The Erotic Mind. Jack Morin. (Harper Perennial 1995)

The Glance: Rumi's Songs of Soul-Meeting. Rumi. Translated by Coleman Barks. (Penguin Books 1999)

The Gnostic Gospels. Elaine Pagels. (Random House 1989)

The Gospel of Mary Magdalene. Jean-Yves Leloup. (Inner Traditions 2002)

Growing Up Again. Jean Illsey Clarke & Connie Dawson. (Hazeldon 1989)

Healing Into Life and Death. Stephen Levine. (Anchor Books 1987)

The Heart of Relationship. Jonathan Goodman-Herrick. (Firstbooks 2002)

I Heard God Laughing. Hafiz-trans. Daniel Ladinsky. (Sufism Reoriented 1996)

Jung on Evil. Edited by Murray Stein. (Princeton University Press 1995)

The Kabbalah of Creation. Isaac Luria, translated with commentary Eliahu Klein. (Jason Aronson 2000)

Kabbalah and Consciousness. Alan Afterman. (Sheep Meadow Press 1992)

Kabbalah and Psychology. Z'Ev Ben Shimon Halevi. (Gateway Publishing 1987)

Practical Kabbalah. Laibl Wolf. (Three Rivers Press 1999)

The Magic of the Ordinary. Gershon Winkler. (North Atlantic Books 2003)

Man's Quest for God. Abraham Joshua Heschel. (Reprinted by Aurora Press 1998)

Meditation and Kabbalah. Aryeh Kaplan. (Jason Aronson 1995)

Meeting the Shadow. Ed. Connie Zwieg & Jeremiah Abrams (Jeremy Tarcher 1991)

The Nag Hammadi Library. Ed. James Robinson (Harper Collins 1988)

A Return To Love. Maryanne Williamson. (Harper Collins 1993)

The Rainbow Bridge. Two Disciples. (Triune Foundation 1981)

The Receiving: Reclaiming Jewish Women's Wisdom. Rabbi Tirzah Firestone. (Harper San Francisco 2003)

The Shadow of the Object: Psychoanalysis of the Unknown Thought. Christopher Bollas. (Columbia University Press 1987)

The Subject Tonight Is Love: 60 Wild and Sweet Poems by Hafiz. Hafiz. Translated by Daniel Ladinsky (Sheriar Press 1996).

The Teachings of Kebzeh: Essentials of Sufism From The Caucausus Mountains. Murat Yagan. Edited by Ya'qub Ibn Yusuf. (Kebzeh Publications 1995).

Theatres of the Body. Joyce Macdougal. (Norton Books 1989).

This Is For Everyone: Universal Principles of Healing Prayer and the Jewish Mystics. Douglas Goldhammer & Melinda Stengel. (Larson Publications 1999)

Treatise of the Pool. Obadiyah Maimonides translated with commentary Dr. Paul Fenton (The Sufi Trust 1981)

The Unfettered Mind. Tahuan Soho. Translated by William Scott Wilson (Kodo Publications 1989)

When Things Fall Apart. Pema Chodron (Shamballa 1997)

With Roots In Heaven. Rabbi Tirzah Firestone. (Plume 1998)

About the Author

About the Author

Dr. Jodi Shams Prinzivalli is the founder and director of the Center for Healing and Energetic Psychology with offices and classes in Northern New Jersey, Manhattan and Chicago. She is a naturopathic physician, a transpersonal psychologist and a conflict resolution specialist. Traditionally trained in clinical psychology, she is also a Kabbalistic Healer, and Certified Addictions Counselor, a Certified Eating Disorders Therapist and a Certified Hypnotherapist.

In addition, she has been trained extensively in the Sufi and Kabbalistic traditions in both Jerusalem, Israel and the United States. Using an eclectic approach to living an awakened life, Dr. Prinzivalli weaves the best of the ancient traditions with cutting edge skills for healing the unconscious mind.

She is also involved in several projects related to interfaith dialogue among the Abrahamic traditions of the Middle East and is the New York coordinator for the Interfaith Encounter Association.

Her life and work is dedicated to bringing forward the original teachings of the sages, making them culturally relevant and grounded in the modern world, weaving them with psychospiritual development, and restoring the Divine Feminine into the psyche of humanity. She now divides her time between private practice; workshop facilitation in Voice Dialogue/ShadowWork and Kabbalistic Psychology/Healing; and interfaith work in New York, Jerusalem, and Istanbul.

To contact Dr. Prinzivalli directly, please visit www.energeticpsychology.com Or e-mail directly at jodiprinz@optonline.net

To be part of our virtual community, please visit yahoogroups.com and click on practicalmystics@yahoogroups.com

CPSIA information can be obtained
at www.ICGtesting.com
Printed in the USA
LVOW12*0019280717

542944LV00006B/35/P